They Also Serve

Bob Sharpe, who was born in 1902 and died in 1985, worked both in London and in several country houses.

Tom Quinn is the editor of the *Country Landowner's Magazine*. He has spent the past twenty years interviewing people who worked in domestic service, getting them to tell him their life stories.

They Also Serve

Bob Sharpe
written with Tom Quinn

CORONET

First published in Great Britain in 2012 by Coronet
An imprint of Hodder & Stoughton
An Hachette UK company

First published in paperback in 2012

1

A CIP catalogue record for this title is
available from the British Library

ISBN 978 1 444 73592 5
Printed and bound by CPI Group (UK) Ltd, Croydon, CR0 4YY

Hodder & Stoughton policy is to use papers that are
natural, renewable and recyclable products and made
from wood grown in sustainable forests. The logging and
manufacturing processes are expected to conform to the
environmental regulations of the country of origin.

Hodder & Stoughton Ltd
338 Euston Road
London NW1 3BH

www.hodder.co.uk

Chapter 1

I worked for forty years and more in all kinds of houses, including houses so big you could get lost in them. Just before the Great War I started as a hall boy and by the 1950s I was a butler, so in the servant world I went from bottom to top. I was a gentleman's gentleman – a valet – for a few years in the middle of my career but you needed danger money for that sort of work so I got out as soon as I could and went back to being a butler.

As hall boy, garden boy, footman, valet and butler I had to put up with all sorts of nonsense from the people I worked for – childish behaviour, tantrums, and ridiculous demands at all hours of the day and night and often for things you wouldn't like to tell your mother about! But you might also become very close to the man or woman you worked for. And later in my career the barriers seemed to come down completely and employers began to treat me as if I was a friend. They'd sometimes be terrified if you told them you were leaving and would do almost anything to keep you.

A good butler was supposed to be deaf and blind. I had to pretend not to know anything about it when my boss slipped along the corridor and went into the bedroom of another man's wife. Since they were all at it perhaps it didn't much signify, but it was worth being discreet as the butler was the best-paid servant in the house and the less you saw and heard the bigger the tips!

As a butler you had the best of all the servants' rooms. You might even get a house or a flat to yourself. You were treated with great respect by the other servants and sometimes even by the people you worked for. The trick with being a butler was to be aloof without being haughty, distant and unflappable but never rude. Employers loved you to be haughty even if it meant that sometimes it almost began to look as if you were looking down your nose at your social superiors. That's no doubt where the whole Jeeves idea began. A butler who had all sorts of practical abilities and bags of common sense might easily make his boss look like a dithering incompetent.

But all this was in the distant unimaginable future when I was born on an old-fashioned Hertfordshire estate in 1902.

Chapter 2

My dad was a gamekeeper as his father had been. My mother had been born in a village a mile from the big house but still on the estate. She had started as a scullery maid on an estate farm when she was thirteen. So my parents knew all about working in service, but in that special way you only ever found on big estates. By special I mean you really did feel you were part of a big, extended family – not necessarily a happy family, it is true, but a family all the same.

Dad and Mum had known each other at the village school and married in their twenties with the sanction of the estate owner – that was the only way you could do it. You had to ask permission and if the boss thought it was an unsuitable match you didn't argue. You didn't get wed. It wasn't as bad as it was in France a century earlier. Apparently, every servant who wanted to get married had to let his wife-to-be sleep with the boss before the marriage. At least we'd got past that!

Of course the day she got married my mother had

to stop work completely – I mean paid work of course – because that was the way things were done then. Married women generally weren't allowed to work although you did occasionally get a husband and wife team where the cook, who might double as the house-keeper, was married to the butler or steward and they'd have married quarters, but I'd say that was rare. My mother used to say, 'Give up work, that's a bloody joke. Working in service was easy compared to looking after you lot and your dad!'

I had two older brothers who both became keepers and they stayed at keepering most of their lives. I was closest to Bill who died during the Second War. The irony is he was too old for active service but had an accident while out shooting. He fell into an old marl pit and fractured his skull. His brain swelled and he had a very painful death I think. Roger, my other brother, worked till after the Second War on the estate and then went to work at a plant nursery for his last few years. He died in the mid 1950s. I was the only brother who went into the house to work. I'm not sure anyone felt that going into the house was a good thing or a better thing than staying as a keeper. In fact, probably the opposite.

But there was never any question that I would work somewhere on the estate. There was nothing else to do anyway and my father would have been offended at the idea that his sort of work wasn't good enough for me. There was none of that business of him wanting me to be better than he was, or get an education and go away from the estate. Good heavens, no. He thought being a keeper or a forester or any job on a big estate was the greatest thing in the world. His father had worked on the estate and he was proud that he himself had carried on and that his sons would carry on. The tradition was everything.

In those days before the Great War when the rich were taxed very little I reckon every county had thirty or forty big houses each with a staff of at least thirty or forty. Who would have dreamed that in my lifetime all that would pass away? We thought it would last forever.

Chapter 3

I learned to read and write at the local school but I must admit that going to school at all seemed silly to me at the time because I knew I would be working with my father when I left and nothing we learned at school seemed relevant. We didn't learn about rearing pheasants or catching stoats! But I stayed in school because my father knew I might need to write a letter for a job now and then. It would also have looked bad to the people we worked for if any of their servants were completely illiterate.

We only learned to read and write at school. No science, not much maths – and little reading beyond the Bible. There was a still an idea that you had to know your place and what was the point of a gamekeeper's boy learning highfalutin stuff? All that was for people far above us. No one questioned things in those days. We were born a generation too soon for that.

We had some laughs at school, though. I remember my mate Billy Freely who was always being whacked by the master. Billy was a right little rogue but a genius for finding birds' eggs in the hedges. Anyway, he hated school and always misbehaved. One day the master really laid into him. Billy tried to cover his head as the blows rained down and then we all heard him shout, 'Are you going to fucking kill me or what?' Well, we couldn't believe it. He was whisked out the door in a second and didn't come back for a week.

I always say I was at school till twelve, which is true, but I actually started to work in the evenings and at weekends when I was about eight. I helped my dad in the pens where the pheasant chicks were reared and by walking about the woods checking the traps for stoats and shooting crows and other vermin. By vermin we meant the sort of animals that might eat the young pheasants or their eggs or the food we left out for the adult birds.

Pheasant rearing was sometimes a brutal business in the pens and hatcheries. We'd just pinch the heads of weaker chicks which crushed their skulls. They'd be no good so they had to be got rid of. The older keepers used to bite the backs of their heads in a second but I couldn't bring myself to do that.

I learned to shoot with a 16-bore shotgun at about eight. A 16-bore is a lighter gun than the standard 12-bore and good for youngsters. That first day with a gun was the strictest training day of my life. My father's face was more serious than I'd ever seen it. He leaned down and looked right into my face and said: 'You can't make a mistake with a gun, not even once, or someone will be killed.'

He then sat me down at the back of our cottage and made me put the gun together and take it apart until he was happy I could do it with my eyes shut. It's not that difficult – the fore-end (the slim bit of wood under the barrels that you rest your hand on when shooting) clips off and then the barrels come away from the action and the stock. Simple. Then came lesson number two. He told me that if he ever saw me carrying the gun closed when I wasn't shooting he'd give me a good whipping – and he would have done it. If you weren't walking along ready to shoot or standing in line waiting for birds to come over, you always had to open your gun and carry it open. Always. And if someone handed you a closed gun you were immediately to open it to check it wasn't loaded. Strict rules, you see. There were terrible accidents occasionally because people didn't stick to the rules. And there were many equally strict rules I was to learn in other areas of service during my long years in various houses. But the rules of shooting I learned first.

I started to help with the Saturday shoots while still at school – shoot days for the guests up at the house were usually Wednesdays and Saturdays. We'd walk miles beating with sticks through dense thickets and brambles to push the pheasants up over the Guns. Pheasants are lazy birds and when they heard us coming towards them stretched out in a long line they would run forward rather than take to the air straight away. Some would try to run back through the line of beaters, but all the others would reach the edge of the wood eventually and knowing they couldn't run back past the beaters they would at last take to the air and sail over the guns waiting in the valley below the wood. A team of twelve guns might kill a thousand birds in a day like this. The point was the so-called sport – the skill of hitting the high birds as they came over. If, at the end of the day, the price for pheasants was too low and it would cost more to get them to market than you'd get back from selling them then they'd bury the whole lot in a big pit – wasn't that terrible? Bury them rather than give them away and God knows there were enough deserving poor round about who could have done with a bird or two. But there was an idea, a leftover I think from the eighteenth century, that game was for the gentry and not for the poor so they shouldn't be given it, although the keepers and beaters might be given a brace now and then.

The boss, the landowner my dad worked for I mean, would always invite his friends for the shooting which went roughly from October to February. His friends were other county types with their own estates, the bigger farmers from round about or businessmen and politicians from London. We also had lords and sometimes a foreign bigwig. They were the landowner's friends and acquaintances and he knew he would be invited back to their shoots. No one paid for anything himself. It was all by invitation. Through the season the boss and his sons might shoot two or three days a week, as well as hunt. This was how they filled the winter months. They wouldn't have dreamt of playing golf or tennis – that was for people in the suburbs.

In the spring a third or half the servants would move to the London house where the family went to the theatre and to dine at each other's houses. In August they would go to Scotland for the grouse shooting. And again many of the staff went with them or went up earlier than the family to get things ready.

But the extent to which my family was part of the estate can be judged by the fact that two of my uncles were gardeners there and my great-grandfather had been a keeper in the early nineteenth century when they still used muzzle-loaders – guns that had to be loaded down the barrels rather than the breech-loaders that were used in my time. We had a photo of great-granddad in old age in his moleskin trousers standing by the gibbet – that was the place where the keeper nailed up all the dead animals he had trapped and shot. They were usually nailed to a shed door or hooked along a wire fence and they hung there till they rotted away. The idea was to show the boss if he had a walk round that you were doing your job!

My mum used to tell us about being a skit in the kitchen. By skit she meant the last-in maid who did all the worst work, washing the floors, peeling vege-tables, cleaning boots and shoes. She used to say she was scared half to death when she first went into the little cubbyhole where she was expected to work and sleep. None of the other servants did a thing when they heard her crying.

'We had to eat terrible things sometimes,' she said. 'We had pig's cheeks one day and the pig's eye was still attached but I didn't care, I was starving. I'd have eaten the pig's ears if there had been nothing else!'

I helped with the harvest along with all the village and estate lads. As the reaper went round the field and the standing corn became a tiny island in the middle, there'd be a great rush of rats and corncrakes and mice and rabbits desperate to escape. We'd try to hit them with sticks, men would shoot at them, dogs would chase them. It was chaos and we loved it. It was a miracle we never killed each other in our excitement.

Chapter 4

But then I got a shock when I left school for good. Instead of starting work as a keeper's lad, which is what I'd expected, I was given a job in the big house as a hall boy. As I've said, my dad didn't think it was better to work in the house than as a keeper or farm worker. It was just that he was offered a job for me and I took it because if I hadn't Dad's boss would have been furious. When you were offered a job it wasn't really an offer at all. You took what you were given. The landowner would have taken it as insolence if you'd hummed and hawed about whether you wanted it or not. The other lads, including poor Billy Freely, thought I was lucky because at least I wouldn't be out in all weathers. Billy went on the land as a plough boy. A terribly hard life.

Anyway, I remember my first day in the big house. It wasn't a great aristocratic mansion such as Chatsworth or anything like it, but I reckon there were twenty bedrooms, two or three book rooms and endless billiard rooms, drawing rooms and sitting rooms not to mention all the servants' rooms. It was an ugly, inconvenient Victorian house, demolished in the 1950s.

There were strict rules about what you could and couldn't do as a hall boy – the hall referred to the servants' hall not the grand entrance hall to the house. I was told I was never to go upstairs unless instructed to, never to use or go near the front door unless instructed to and never to speak to any member of the family in the unlikely event of meeting one of them. I was also told to ask the maids if I needed help and not the cook or the butler or footman or anyone else.

You have to remember that even quite small country houses before the Great War were designed to ensure as little contact between servants and their employers as possible. It was a very strict rule but strict rules existed at every level – that's why I couldn't ever speak to the butler or the cook. I was too lowly and even the servants wanted their status.

We knew nothing else in those days. We accepted our lot and I don't really remember hearing anyone question the right of people to have servants and treat them harshly.

My job as hall boy meant cleaning a lot of shoes and boots. I sometimes did the gentlemen's hunting boots and their shoes but mostly I was cleaning the upper servants' shoes and boots. I did the butler's and the footmen's, and with the scullery maid I had to empty all the chamber pots every morning There might be twenty or thirty of these if you added all the servants and the family and visitors. I remember once early on when I hadn't really got the hang of it I made the mistake on a freezing winter morning of running across the yard carrying a chamber pot. I slipped and fell and the contents went all over me.

I'd only been doing the job for about a month. The kitchen maid was very grumpy and told to clean me up. She never said a word or caught my eye but she picked up a broom and used it to push me to the middle of the yard. She told me to stand still and then went back in the kitchen. She came back out with a tin bucket filled with water and threw it over me. The shock made me slip on the cobbles and down I went again. But I noticed that the water wasn't ice cold as it should have been – just as well as this was January.

'I warmed it up a bit with the kettle,' said the maid, who winked at me, smiled, and marched off. I would never have cried at this sort of treatment because you got it all the time when you were at the bottom of the pile. And I had to work the rest of my sixteen-hour day in wet clothes which didn't dry off till late that evening. The tops of my legs were bleeding from the chaffing of the wet cloth, but the pain and humiliation meant I'd learned my lesson. I did everything with the greatest care after that.

Chapter 5

To a youngster, all older people seem a bit dotty. I'd seen the funny habits of the various estate staff, especially keepers and beaters, while I'd helped my dad, but being hall boy introduced me to the eccentricities of the indoor servants and even the wealthy people we worked for.

My day as hall boy started at five o'clock. I was still living at home at this point. We never had an alarm clock but when you have to get up in the morning it is surprising how quickly you learn to do it automatically. I'd hop out of my bed, get a piece of bread and butter if there was any from the kitchen and eat it as I ran quickly across two small fields to the house. The servants' door was at the back and it gave on to a cobbled yard that was surrounded by low buildings on three sides. These buildings were filled with upended dog carts riddled with woodworm, old barrels, old saddles and farm implements and I once found a stack of oil paintings covered in bird droppings and dust. They still had their ornate gilt frames and I've often wondered since if they were valuable. One showed cattle coming down to a lake in the mountains to drink. It was beautifully done but perhaps a little unfashionable which is why it had ended up in an outbuilding. Pictures often went from the drawing room to an old passage and then to the servants' corridors and finally to the barn!

The kitchen maid and scullery maid were always already at work when I nipped in the door and made my way to the servants' hall, which was just a big room where the servants ate round a giant table. Off the hall was the big kitchen, then the laundry room and up a short flight of stairs the butler's pantry. I was never allowed in the butler's pantry. This is where the family silver was kept. The family only ate off solid silver. It wasn't the grandest family in the county by any means but eating off silver was a status thing and no family worth its salt would eat off anything less.

The butler's room led into the pantry and the butler was responsible for making sure the silver wasn't stolen. He and the footmen also had to keep it all clean. The upper staff had their meals in there with the silver, served by the lower staff.

So you see we were a little world cut off from the rest of humanity but to this day I have no idea where the family got its money. It was probably inherited and land-based, given to them for fighting on some medieval battlefield for the winning side.

A few things I discovered about his lordship were perhaps the stuff of gossip but, despite that, I'm sure they were true. Every January he was reputed to give up smoking and drinking and to walk around with half a raw cabbage in his pocket. Whenever he was hungry he would whip out the cabbage and take a bite. In January, too, he insisted that his bed be moved every few days – he had the footmen carry it from drawing room to bedroom and back again. As soon as February came he stayed in his bedroom, took up his tobacco again and presumably threw away what was left of his cabbage.

My first job when I got into the hall at about ten past five was to go to the boot room and start cleaning. The scullery maid would leave the shoes there or I might go and collect them from outside the butler's room, the cook's room, the footmen's and the house-keeper's rooms. We used a special beeswax cream that came in big tins but there was spit and polish and elbow grease too. You got a good shine by really going over the leather well with brushes and then cloths. If they weren't absolutely perfect there was hell to pay. But the boots were only the beginning – in fact it was the easy bit because at least I could sit on a stool to do it. Once the boots were cleaned the fun really started!

I would have to run to the wood store which was across the cobbled courtyard and get a wheelbarrow full of logs. I'd then take these in small batches in a box with a handle up the servants' stairs and into the drawing rooms, the sitting rooms and billiard rooms. I would only put the logs in the log baskets because it was the job of the footmen to light the fires and keep them going.

It used to make me laugh that members of the family wouldn't even give the fire a poke to liven it up. They would always ring for the footman to do it and of course to put more logs on the fire. In some houses the footman might spend the whole evening standing in the sitting room in case anything needed to be done and he'd be listening to all sorts of intimate family conversations. When I became a footman I heard the most outrageous things, but they liked footmen who could look like marble for hours on end.

I did all the carrying of firewood at a run because otherwise I knew I wouldn't get it done in time. Once the family had left their bedrooms and were at breakfast I would have to carry wood up to their rooms and to the butler's, housekeeper's and footmen's rooms. It was a terrible carry-on, a terrible rush, and the cook I remember would give me a terrific smack around the head if ever I got in her way while crossing the kitchen. I had to run through the kitchen many times in a day and there was an art to dashing through without getting a clout round the ear – and the cook wasn't giving friendly taps. I never quite mastered it but after a while avoided being hit every time. She would really try to belt you and if she hit you on the ear you'd be deaf for half the day afterwards. Why Cook always felt she had to belt me I never discovered because I was never allowed to speak to her. She often hit the scullery maid and kitchen maid too. She was ferociously bad-tempered. Once she threw a saucepan at me but luckily it was empty – and she missed. I don't think she ever said a kind word to anyone but she was a very good cook apparently. I was told later on that when her son was killed in the Great War she only took an afternoon off for his funeral and was back cooking the following day. She never shed a tear in front of a soul.

All the time I was hall boy I did sixteen-hour days seven days a week, but with a half-day off at Christmas.

It was a terrible job that made any job you did later in service seem like heaven in comparison. I did it for eight years with no time off at all. I was lucky I didn't have to sleep in the house. I went home after my sixteen-hour day and fell into bed. Most hall boys had to sleep in the servants' hall – just on a small cheap mattress in a cupboard or cellar and they wouldn't be expected to change out of their clothes for weeks at a time. They might keep them on for a month.

I swear some of the men whose boots I cleaned thought they reappeared each morning by magic. I never cleaned her ladyship's shoes or his lordship's. They were always cleaned by the footmen, the lady's maid or the valet.

Other jobs for the hall boy included scrubbing the yards with a broom and water every day, sprinkling water on the yards in summer to lay the dust and scrubbing the passageways and kitchen floors as well as pretty much anything anyone needed. In other words I was a dogsbody and when someone shouted 'Get a tin of polish,' or 'Clean that window,' or 'Get some more coals,' I was off like a shot. You wanted to be good at your job even if you were at the bottom of the pile like me because that was the only way to rise in the world. My attitude helped me eventually become a footman and then a butler quicker than many managed it.

Once a week I received a small package from one of the housemaids. This contained two pairs of the butler's flannel drawers that I was supposed to iron. I'm sure the housemaids were supposed to do it, but they always gave it to me. I just used to grab an iron from the range where they were kept warm almost continually. I ran it quickly over the drawers before putting them back in the brown paper and leaving them on the servants' hall table for the maid to return.

Anyway I worked on the shoes and boots and fires and chamber pots and drawers till I was sick of the sight of them and then, out of the blue, I was told they needed a garden boy and that was me. No one asked if I minded the change. I just had to do it and it was to be quite a while before I went back into the house.

Chapter 6

The garden boy was just a general outside dogsbody working in a huge garden where there were dozens of tasks to do all day every day even in the depths of winter. I reckon the garden covered more than two or three acres and it was walled all the way round so that delicate vegetables and fruit could be grown. The growing season was much longer because of that big old wall. I reckon it was ten feet tall and it kept the winds off and protected the plants from frost. We grew melons under glass, and oranges, but my memory of my time in the garden is all filled with the smell of horse manure because I seemed to spend most of my time carting it around. We must have used twenty tonnes of the stuff each year.

The old gardener was known to everyone as Mister Kent. He was the first servant I'd met who took any interest at all in me beyond giving me a belt for getting in the way. He wore a straw hat even in winter which was very daring for those times because people were sticklers for wearing the right thing to suit their station in life and the time of year. If you wore a straw hat in London in winter you would be stared at. You might even be jeered and jostled.

'I'm not a gentleman, that's why I wear it wrong,' Mister Kent used to say in a thick Hertfordshire accent. I haven't heard this accent since before the Second World War. We were close to London and many Londoners came here during the fighting. Afterwards the accent became a sort of softened cockney. But old Kent had the old country accent of my part of the world. He called magpies pikeys too – the word that had become a name for gipsies – but he used it and lots of other words too in the old way. He was a crafty but lovely old bugger and whenever I'd finished a job and went back to him for the next job he'd sit me down and say, 'Ten minutes on your bum, son. Git down there, you're making me tired with yer fizzin'.' He meant that I was running around too much.

'How much horse shit do you think you've moved the day?' he'd ask me. 'Come on, how much?'

'Eight barrow-loads and I've ten more at least to move,' I'd reply.

'Do you know where all that shit goes?' he'd ask while hunting for the kettle through all sorts of piles of rubbish.

'Where does it go, Mister Kent?' I'd reply.

'It goes into the guts of my lord and lady fuckin' layabout!'

With that old Kent would start rocking back and

forth on his heels and laughing. Then he'd make a terrible noise in his throat and spit a gobbet almost the size of a golf ball twenty feet out through the door into the garden.

'Beat that if you can,' he'd then say. The first time I heard this I just smiled but he said, 'Go on, have a try at it.'

I tried but my effort was poor.

'What the hell was that supposed to be?' he asked. 'I'll show you how to do it.'

And then he proceeded to explain the art of distance spitting as if he was teaching me higher mathematics.

'You need to get smoking, twenty Capstan a day at least, because you need plenty of solid phlegm. Roll it round in your mouth and then put it just back from the tip of your tongue. Then take a deep breath and make a small shape like a zero with your mouth and blow for all you're worth. You see, the narrow mouth forces the air – turns you mouth into an airgun. I'm a fuckin genius aren't I? Wasted in this bloody garden.'

All the time he was saying this sort of thing he would laugh and gasp, but all the while he had one eye keeping lookout through the doors of his shed to make sure no one was coming. If he saw one of the under-gardeners outside his shed he'd spin his hat out at them or throw a potato at them. He was always in high spirits and was the first person I met who really knew how to enjoy himself. My father like most men at that time was much more serious, whereas old Kent took nothing at all seriously. But he was a brilliant gardener who could take a battered little cutting from any plant and make it grow at a terrific speed. His various projects round the garden produced huge amounts of vegetables and fruit and whenever I asked him how he did it he'd always say, 'It's down to the quality of the dung, sir.'

He would say the most outrageous things but because he said them in a straightforward way it was very hard for anyone to take offence. He was one of the few servants I came across in my career who seemed in many ways far cleverer than the people he worked for despite his complete lack of formal education.

The thing about old Kent was that he had found a way to be himself with his social superiors. He thought the fact that they didn't quite know how to deal with him was huge fun. It gave him a dignity that very few servants ever had. I certainly never had it. Another very strange thing about old Kent was that the lady of the house would come down deliberately now and then to talk to him and they talked almost like old friends. He never seemed to defer to her in manner or speech at all, which amazed me. The truth was she really liked old Kent which is why she broke the rules and came to see him. She couldn't help herself. Once I saw her coming along the path towards his little shed.

'Shall I make myself scarce?' I asked.

'You will not,' he said. 'I'll introduce you!'

Kent brushed the dust off an old chair that had no back and invited her to sit down. He then chatted away about the flowers and the vegetables as if he was every bit her equal. I sat absolutely still in the corner shadows terrified I'd be noticed.

Then he said, 'Shall we go see the repairs to the glasshouse? They've done a lovely job. Lovely.'

'Yes of course,' said her ladyship and up she got, ready to go at his bidding.

'Oh, this is my young friend Bob,' said old Kent suddenly turning back to face me. 'He's the garden boy and a great lad. The best we've had.'

I learned later that she was the rebel of the family and hated all the stuffiness and etiquette involved in doing the few things that, as a lady, she was allowed to do. She liked old Kent, that was obvious. But seeing him and talking to him the way she did clearly also appealed to the rebel in her because it would certainly have been frowned on by the rest of the family.

She didn't exactly smile at me as we were introduced, but I whipped off my cap and nodded and she nodded back and then looked at old Kent with a really big smile. It was in that moment I realised what a special relationship they had. I was delighted at the way he'd praised me but it was typical of Kent. My dad would never have said such a thing. I can remember Dad slapped me once for crying when I was about six so I never did it again in his presence. Kent would never have done that. He found me crying once but only because I was exhausted, and without saying a word made me a cup of tea, patted me on the head and pointed to a great mass of straw kept right at the back of his shed for the strawberries.

'Sit on that straw and have your tea over there,' he said, so I sat on the straw and in a second was fast asleep. He woke me up half an hour later and said, 'Quick now, Katy's coming.' It was the maid come to look for me.

'Where the hell is that boy?' she said as she appeared in the doorway.

'Now Katy, keep yer bonnet on,' said Kent soothingly, 'I've had him here helping with a dozen things. I'm workin' 'im to death so it's not his fault he didn't come up to the house, it's my fault, so you can just give me a good clip round the ear.'

'Get off you cheeky devil,' said Katy. 'If you wait a minute I *will* give you a clout.'

Then she looked at me and said: 'Come on you, the rabbits are waiting to be boiled.'

Boiling the rabbits was something I had to do every few days. They were shot all the time round the estate because in those days there were millions of them and they were a terrible pest. They were hated not so much because they ate the crops but because they urinated on them. Whole patches of the fields near their burries would be brown because their urine was so strong. It killed everything.

Anyway the keepers and estate lads shot them as often as they could, as I had once done with my dad, and they were then carted up to the house. A few were kept for the kitchen but the rest, after they'd been skinned, went into the dog food boiler. The skins were sold and the money went to the kitchen maid – a few shillings only but she'd be glad to have it.

The smell of boiling rabbit meat was appalling which is why they were boiled in a giant pot on an open fire well away from the house. I threw the carcases in and pushed them around in the hot water till the meat fell off the bones. I'd then take the bucket of meat to the various keepers and feed their dogs – there were dogs everywhere on the estate, including four Labradors kept specially for his lordship. If the dogs had an unvarying diet, it was worse for the local pack of foxhounds – they got all the offal that had been condemned as unfit for humans from the slaughterhouse. It was usually condemned because the cattle and pigs from which it came were ill, usually with tuberculosis, when killed.

Old Kent knew everything about dogs and hounds and had some great stories about his own youth on the estate. He'd been a cartridge boy, for example. This was a highly skilled job that involved keeping four shotgun cartridges wedged between your fingers until the loader needed them. The cartridge boy would give them to the loader who put them in his master's gun and then passed the gun to the master. At that very moment the master would be handing back the gun he'd just fired (and which was empty) to the loader who would then reach back for the cartridge boy to hand him two more cartridges.

It sounds pretty straightforward but when hundreds of birds were rocketing over your heads at forty miles an hour, it had all to be done at high speed. Cartridge boys often had to go back to the kitchen or the yard because they couldn't get the hang of it. They hated being sacked like that because they missed out on the tips and guns were always more of a draw than boot cleaning. But the gentlemen shots prided themselves not just on their accuracy but on their speed and that depended on the speed of the cartridge boy and the loader. Some teams were legendary. From a previous generation the Indian shot Maharajah Duleep Singh, a great friend of Queen Victoria's, had a very good team, at least that's what Kent told me.

'He came here in the 1870s. Mad about shooting he was, but he was a rum 'un too. Used to turn up in full Highland dress – full kilt, dirk, the bloody lot. But he was thick as thieves with the old Queen. I reckon she was in love with him. Used to call him the Black Prince of Perthshire!'

Kent had been a very good cartridge boy, at least by his own account, and he claimed he'd helped out when the Prince of Wales, later Edward VII, was shooting and his usual cartridge boy was absent.

'He was an idiot,' said Kent. 'Fit for nothing but chasing women and eating. I've seen more brains in an onion, but I felt sorry for him later on when I read how his mother, that old bitch Victoria, had treated him when he was a lad. She mocked him and told him he was useless till he believed it and she was ashamed of him. She made him wear irons on his legs to make him walk straight. I saw him at a shoot lunch and thought he'd burst he ate and drank so much, and he was definitely drunk when he went back to shoot that afternoon. He really thought he had great abilities too because even when he missed every bird in sight people pretended he was knocking them out of the sky like Annie Oakley.'

This was shocking to me who had only heard the royal family praised to the skies by everyone. No one in those days ever uttered a word of criticism about them, but Kent was a maverick if ever there was one and I loved him for it.

He was a great man for stories about the royals who he seemed partly to admire and partly to detest. My favourite story was about Edward VII.

'Oh yes you got your money's worth with him. Bit of a practical joker. I'll give you an example. He always brought along a loader who was the same height and build as himself. The loader had a beard just like the king's, too, and wore almost the same clothes. The king thought it was a great joke because the flunkeys would sometimes get confused and bow and scrape to the wrong man!'

Chapter 7

When one of the stable lads had bullied me Kent found the solution. I told him the boy used to find a reason to hit me every time we found ourselves in the same part of the yard or garden. Now my father would have looked angrily at me for being too weak to stand up for myself if i'd told him, but old Kent winked at me and said, 'I'll sort that little bastard don't you worry.' I had no idea at the time what he did or said but next time I saw the stable lad he was as nice as pie. He said, 'Here, have a biscuit,' and handed me a piece of shortbread which was a great treat. Then he asked if I wanted to go looking for birds' eggs. I was amazed.

Later I found out from another stable lad that Kent had spoken in awe of my deadliness in a fight and that though I was a quiet one, once roused I didn't stop. He said I'd broken a lad's jaw in a fight and put two others in hospital!

Old Kent was a great source of poaching stories. He himself had done a bit of poaching as a boy, he explained to me.

'My brother and me would get up very early and take a few pages from a newspaper and cut them into eight-inch squares. We twisted the squares into little cone-shaped packets and fitted them together one inside the other and popped them inside a sack.

'Then we took a thick, sharp-pointed iron bar about two feet long and a small bottle of birdlime – a sort of sticky glue. We then went off to the fields by the pheasant woods. My brother kept a lookout and I went off across the field towards the edge of the first wood. Twenty yards from the trees I'd whip out the poker and make a dozen holes in the ground round about. I'd then put a paper cone into each hole and tip in a few grains of barley. Then came the clever bit. I'd paint a line of birdlime round the edge of the paper cone.

'Pheasants will always run away from a stranger, but if they see him lingering near their home wood, especially if he stoops much of the time, they will keep their eyes fixed on him and the minute he goes they will come out to investigate what he's been up to. So having fitted the cones in their little holes I'd go back to my brother hiding in the hedge and we'd wait. Within half an hour a few pheasants would come cautiously out to sun themselves and start tap tapping away at the barley I'd sprinkled all around the holes and the cones. Pheasants get addicted to barley and soon they'd be poking and pecking everywhere. Eventually one would put its head into a cone and when it lifted it out again it would find a cone firmly attached to its head. If it can't see, a pheasant will go quiet and make no attempt to fly. Within ten minutes we'd have three or four pheasants quietly walking around with paper cones on their heads waiting to be picked up!'

When I heard old Kent's tales of shooting and poaching I longed to be a cartridge boy rather than a garden boy but I think I was safer in the garden. 'You couldn't make a single mistake or fumble the cartridges,' said Kent, 'or you'd be sent home in disgrace. Terrible pressure.'

But I did see an unusual bit of shooting on one occasion after I was asked to clear up after a pigeon competition. This competition wasn't with wild pigeon it was semi-tame birds – and very cruel I think. They'd buy a few hundred feral pigeons, sometimes a thousand or more, and then pull out their tail feathers so they would fly erratically. They'd be kept in a special aviary until the day of the shoot. Then when the great day came each pigeon would be put one by one in a small collapsible box on the ground. The competitors would stand thirty yards away from the box and when they were ready they would shout and one of the servants would pull a string running from the box to a far corner out of range of the guns. As the string was pulled the box would collapse and the poor bird, minus its tail feathers, would try to fly off. Nine times out of ten before a bird was ten feet off the ground it would have been shot. The gentlemen would shoot a few hundred pigeon in this way and they usually bet on who would win.

I helped clear up at the end of one pigeon afternoon and I remember we put all the dead birds in a huge wooden box. And what troubles me still is that many of the birds in that huge box were still alive though badly hurt. Having been shot they were suffocated by the weight of all the dead birds on top of them. No one thought anything of it at the time. Animals were there to be eaten, shot for sport or killed for being pests.

After I'd been working as a garden boy for a couple of years, I noticed that poor Kent had lost some of his old sense of fun. He began to lose weight and I remember noticing how yellow his skin had become. He was still very friendly to me all the time I was with him but subdued and quiet. They kept him on till the last which was decent of them but one day I went down to his shed and he wasn't there. I found out later he had died a few days earlier. This was a terrific shock to me who hadn't yet known anyone close who had died. I knew he had been ill but when you're young you think that people who are ill go to the doctor and the doctor makes them better. It was like watching a light fading inside someone. But I was still young and even as he faded it never occurred to me that one day he would no longer be there. I realised how close I had been to him and how drawn I was to his personality by the fact that I missed him so badly. He was such a pleasure to be with that when he was no longer there I felt completely aimless for a while. I still did my work but several times a day found myself wandering unthinkingly down towards his shed, forgetting for the moment that it had been cleared out and all trace of him was gone. On the day I heard he'd died I went to his shed and helped myself to his straw hat – an odd thing to do. I kept it for years afterwards. The sadness left after he died took a long time to fade.

Chapter 8

But life went on and I was kept very busy with long days and little time off. A new gardener came and tidied things up and made us work even harder, and the lady of the house was never seen in the garden again – at least not by me.

By now I was given a little more time off now and then and had afternoons collecting birds' eggs which became a passion of mine. Other times when I was given the afternoon off I was too tired to do anything but sleep, which led to one very embarrassing incident. I had a spare couple of hours and decided to go and lie down in an empty stable to try to get some sleep. There was a long range of beautiful red-brick stables that were much older than the house itself with room for ten or more horses. Soon I was fast asleep and then in my dream it was raining and the rain got worse and I was afraid I'd drown. But even in my dream I sensed there was something mysterious and odd about the rain because it was warm and there was so much of it. I woke up with a start to discover that one of the great shire horses used around the estate was having a copious piss all over me.

Chapter 9

With my friend Kent gone I saw a lot more of my brother Bill. We'd always been fairly close and like me he was mad about collecting birds' eggs and fishing. He was four years older than me and his whole working life was keepering and shooting. He was fair with blue eyes while I was darker with brown eyes and at least four inches shorter. He always seemed like a giant to me when I was very young – immensely strong. He would lift two massive sacks of grain as if they were pillows.

He had friends his own age and used to see them now and then in the village pub, but he only ever asked me to fish with him. They were his drinking pals and I was his fishing pal. He used to say, 'Come on, Bob, the roach are biting,' and off we'd go to one of the numerous ponds and lakes around the estate. He always knew when I had an odd few hours off or a whole afternoon and then we'd go after birds or fish.

I remember we once went down to what we used to call the Dead Man's Pool. There were all sorts of rumours about it – that over the centuries dozens of men and women had filled their pockets with stones and walked into its gloomy depths never to be seen again, except on moonlit nights when their white faces would rise up from the depths. Billy and I and the other estate lads thought it was all nonsense until one midsummer night in the early 1920s.

Billy and I had decided to sit by the shore all night to fish for the huge pike that were said to inhabit the lake. I said to Billy:

'Are you sure we'll be all right? Have you stayed all night before?' I asked the question for reassurance although I knew full well he'd never fished the lake at night before. I didn't want to admit it but I was afraid. The lake covered about two acres and was surrounded by thick woodland. Its banks sloped steeply all around and in many places the trees grew right to the edge of the water, which was deep and black.

You could tell how deep it was by the steepness of the banks which ran straight into the water in such a way that there were no shallows at the edges at all. And even on a bright day of sunshine Dead Man's Pool had a forbidding air. There seemed never to be any birds there and because it was in a deep hollow well away from any track or road or farm building it was always eerily quiet.

But Billy was reassuring. 'Don't be daft,' he said, 'it's just a big old pond and no one ever fishes it so we're bound to have all the big ones to ourselves.'

The great day came. It was June and we set off about five o clock in the evening to leave us several hours' fishing before dark. I remember the track wound down across the fields before going more steeply through an old bit of rough pasture. Then we reached the steepest place where the track disappeared into the wood that surrounded the lake. There had been a breeze blowing across the fields during the twenty minutes it had taken us to reach the wood but no sooner had we slipped in among the trees than the wind dropped and not a breath stirred.

Down we went, forcing our way through the bramble clumps, skirting massive old trees that leaned dangerously out over the water that we could now see below us. The path was so steep that we slipped now and then. At the water's edge we found a space and made up a bed of old leaves and bracken to sit on. We set up two big old bamboo rods that Billy had made. This was in the days before fishing tackle could easily be bought ready-made. Only our line and hooks and wooden reels had come from a shop. We swung two small dead fish baits out as far as we could and sat down on our coats, which had been spread out on the bracken bed, to wait. We were trying to catch the big pike that were reputed to haunt the lake. After salmon – and of course there were none of those in the lake – pike was the fish everyone was after in those days. We sat silently but companionably for a couple of hours and then Billy said: 'We'll try for something else. There might be a big old tench out there or a bream.'

He reeled in one of the rods, took off the dead fish and fixed on a smaller hook and a smaller float. He then prised the lid off a huge tin of worms he'd brought with him and put a couple of the biggest worms he could find on the hook before casting out once again.

It grew darker. We ate our bread and butter and waited. In all my life I have never known such silence. No dogs barked in the distance, not a stirring among the branches overhead. Then just as we least expected it one of the reels began gently to click as the line was slowly pulled out by something deep in the lake. We could still see reasonably well though dusk had fallen. Billy crept forward, picked up the rod, counted to three under his breath and then with a great sweep he lifted the rod into the air. Immediately the cane bucked and kicked violently down towards the surface of the water and Billy shouted, 'Got 'im!'

There was a huge silver boil on the surface somewhere out in the lake and the last of the light could be seen glinting on the great fish as it swirled sixty feet out in the darkness. Then the fish made a terrific run across the lake and I could hear the reel screaming and the line singing and Billy cursing. 'Come on you bastard . . . You won't escape this time . . . So you want to make a fight of it. We'll see about that.' And all the time he struggled with the bucking rod and the spinning reel. He told me afterwards that the fish's first run had ripped line off the reel so quickly that when he pressed his palm against the metal reel edge to slow it down his hand was burnt by the friction.

The battle continued with me standing uselessly by, amazed that at last we had hooked a really big fish. On other fishing trips we had only ever caught smaller stuff – roach and bream in one of the other farm lakes.

At last Billy announced that the fish had begun to tire and sure enough we soon saw the big red float coming in as Billy gradually reeled in his leviathan. At the edge of the water I saw a large greeny-silver torpedo that writhed and twisted. When at last it was lying quietly at the edge of the water Billy leaned down and pushed his hand into the fish's gills before triumphantly lifting it clear of the water.

No one put fish back in those days so Billy whacked it on the head with a big stick he found nearby and threw it up the bank behind us. We then did a really odd thing – we embraced each other and did a little dance of joy like modern footballers. Then Billy sat down, pulled out a packet of cigarettes and said: 'I've bloody had it after that!' Meanwhile I went across to the dead fish. It was about two and a half feet long with a great thick ugly head and an extraordinary number of teeth all pointing down its throat.

I had some idea that we would set off for home now as I was still spooked by the strange, still atmosphere by the pool. And by now of course it was as dark as you can imagine. We had no torches and although there was a moon that night it was hidden by the trees and clouds. Billy was excited and would have none of it. 'We can't leave now,' he said. 'There might be armies of giants out there!' I clearly sounded worried so he said, 'Come over here and sit next to me, then we'll have four fists for any ghosts,' and he laughed.

We sat for another hour or more and despite it being midsummer it was cold. By what I estimated to be one or two in the morning we were absolutely freezing. Even Billy admitted he was cold. The utter stillness of the lake and the dark presence of the trees that surrounded it both frightened me and made me sleepy and gradually, though I fought against it, I began to nod off. I'd stopped worrying about the lake being haunted by this time because we'd been there for hours and Billy was close by.

I woke suddenly terrified and found Billy shaking me. I could just make out his eyes in the dark and he looked really scared. 'Listen,' he hissed. I listened and heard the distinct and very loud sound of scratching and snorting and the snorting was echoing around the water.

'Oh Christ,' I said. I whispered in Billy's ear, 'What shall we do?'

He didn't reply but I could feel the tension and terror through his grip on my arm. The two of us sat absolutely rigidly still, listening to the horrible ghostly clanking sounds that seemed to be coming closer with every second that passed. If you'd threatened to shoot me I could not have moved. I was more frightened then than I have ever been since. Neither of us could do a thing for sheer terror and Billy had still not uttered a word.

Then a pale glow grew around us. I forced myself to look up and realised that the moon had come out from behind a cloud and was shining down through a narrow gap in the trees overhead. The unearthly sounds continued and I realised that Billy was making an odd noise and nudging me. I looked at him and followed where he was pointing.

To our relief and amusement we saw our ghost down on the ground and about fifteen feet away. A fat hedgehog was upended in our big worm tin, loudly kicking and scrabbling at the metal edges and greedily finishing the last of our worms.

I had many such days with Billy, who would have been in his mid-twenties at this time. I reckon I was about eighteen. Billy always tried to include me in his fishing expeditions and other adventures despite the fact that I was four years younger, which seemed a lot at the time.

He used to entertain me with some great stories from his work as an under-keeper.

One of my favourites, which he told in a way that would make a dead man laugh, was of a landowner who lived about five miles away. One of Billy's best friends was a keeper there but all the local lads loved to beat there because the landowner always started the day by drinking the beaters' health. Because there was a free drink on offer thirty or forty beaters might turn up where only half that number were needed. But the landowner would never turn anyone away. The beaters would line up by a special table the landowner had set up on the lawn in front the big house. Each beater in turn would be given a small glass of port and the landowner would have one himself. Each beater would be sure to say, 'Your health, sir,' before knocking back the drink. And of course for each drink taken by a beater an equivalent drink would be taken by the landowner until after the fifteenth or sixteenth beater had had his glass the landowner would slowly topple off his chair and be carried insensible into the house.

But not all Billy's stories were funny. He told me once that a very grand visitor who was a notoriously bad and greedy shot had badly injured one of the village boys by shooting too low. The boy had been blinded in one eye and the visitor – who Billy nicknamed Sir Bloody Useless – offered the boy's mother £5 in recompense and was astonished when she indignantly refused. Billy said he heard the man say: 'I offered her generous compensation and she had the effrontery to refuse it. I've done all I can.' What made Billy so cross was the fact that the mother's refusal to take the money became a greater fault than being an unsafe shot who had badly injured a young boy. Typically, too, the visitor continued to be invited each year. 'If it had been a beater shooting and a gentleman's son had been hurt the beater would have hanged,' said Billy.

My father reckoned that the upper classes really

didn't worry too much if they peppered a beater or keeper with shot now and then. He would say: 'When the guests come I always wear a pair of extra-thick corduroys and two coats so the fuckers don't kill me with their bad shooting.'

Billy and old Kent were the two great friends of my youth. Any troubles I had then and later were always made easier because of the laughs I learned to have with them.

But there was one thing Billy would never talk to me about. He had fought in France in the Great War and had come back in 1918 after eighteen months unharmed, which looking back was a bit of a miracle. He hated talking about it and would rarely answer questions, even from me. In fact he would look almost panic-stricken if I asked something so I soon gave up. It was a terrible thing to see him so instantly shaken and upset. The only thing he ever said that I recall now was, 'They cared more about the regimental silver than they cared for us.'

Everyone in the village knew someone who had died in the war but somehow – and I'm embarrassed to admit it – the war seemed too far away to be of great concern to me. I was too young, only twelve when it began, and we were too far away from any big town to hear much news of what was happening. People tell you the whole country thought about nothing else for four years but it's not true. When someone round about lost a son I was too young to understand much about it all. There was no television or radio to show us what was really going on and how awful it was, just the newspapers, which were censored of course, and I never read them and my father hardly ever did. And besides it was all propaganda, wasn't it? The newspapers always made out that we were winning even when things were going very badly. We were forty miles from London but cut off in a way you can't imagine now. Cut off because in those days, with no cars and no money, people stayed at home in their villages for most of their lives and were much less curious about what went on elsewhere than they were once radio came in.

Little changed up at the big house either, or at least little that I would have been aware of. During the war there is no doubt that the very well connected used their influence to make sure that as their servants were called up – only gradually – the nobility were given special treatment. They got to keep more of their servants than others lower down the social scale. I worked in a house that definitely got off lightly because of its connections. In government circles it was felt that the middle classes could manage without their servants but not the delicate upper classes.

I had only two really bad experiences as hall boy. The first of these occurred when I was told by the kitchen maid – the one who'd thrown water all over me when I spilled the chamber pot – that I was to wait by the back door until the butler, Mr Carter, returned from town one evening. The maid had been told by the cook to get me to wait up however long it took because it was Mr Carter's evening off.

So I stood by the back door in the gloomy half light of the corridor while all the other servants gradually went off to bed. I had no idea what time it was but the house fell eerily silent and eventually all I could hear was an occasional scuttle of mice in the ceilings and owls out in the woods. My legs began to ache and I found it hard to stay awake and still Mr Carter did not come. I began to feel really upset that I would not be able to go on much longer and I was shivering with the cold. The next thing I knew I was being shaken awake by one of the housemaids. I said, 'Don't tell Mr Carter I fell asleep.'

'What on earth are you talking about?' she replied. 'Have you been here all night? It's morning, now just get on with your work.' I later discovered that Katie, the maid who had told me to stand there, had been scolded for getting the message wrong. Mr Carter had been in his bed the whole time I had stood at the door and no one had thought to tell me. I hardly know how I got through the day's work after sleeping on the cold floor but I did. The only other time I was really upset was when I was sent fifteen miles on the kitchen bicycle to collect a parcel and had a puncture. I walked almost all the way back in the driving rain, pushing that heavy bike and terrified in case the parcel should get wet.

Chapter 10

I was quite a tall lad and I tried hard to be pleasant to those I worked with. I was never one of those boys who thought of himself as a tough. My mother used to say, 'He's a thinker is Bob,' because I wasn't much interested in sports other than fishing and collecting birds' eggs. I never played football or got into fights like the other village lads. And it was my height and quiet ways I think that led to the offer of a job – another one I couldn't refuse – as a junior footman.

The family were not so grand that there were half a dozen footmen as some houses had, but most county families even up to the Second World War had at least two footmen. We had two and though I was to be junior footman I was really still going to be doing some of the duties of hall boy. I knew that in the late 1800s they'd had as many as four footmen and that they'd stood at the back of the carriage every time it pulled off round the drive. They'd also had to wear powdered horsehair wigs that itched like the devil so I was told. In my time a lot of the pomp had gone because I think there was a manpower shortage and there was definitely less money about with increased taxes even for the very rich.

So it was good to get me cheaply, as I was already nearby and had worked as hall boy and knew the ways of the house.

I must have been around twenty-five, I think, and it all began when I was called up to see the butler, a figure as terrifying as the prime minister or the king. He was called Carter but I was told to call him Mr Carter as all the other servants did. The household – I mean the family members – called him Carter, which wasn't as disrespectful as it might sound because before the First War even young gentlemen who were friendly and knew each other really well still called each other by their surnames.

I was given a day's notice I would need to see Mr Carter to discuss my new position. I was to be outside his pantry where the family silver was kept by 10 a.m., so on the great morning my mother buttoned me carefully into a suit that had been my brother's. It was a little big but no one bothered about that sort of thing in those days. Most poor people wore clothes that were either too small or too big. There was nothing off the peg and only the rich could afford to have a suit specially made for them and taken in and let out as they lost weight or grew bigger. I became an expert on all this sort of thing when I later became a valet and butler.

But on this autumn morning of my interview all I

could think about was what on earth would I say to Mr Carter. I also remember that we didn't have any pomade for my hair. Pomade was very popular then. It was pure grease that you used to plaster down your hair. Very useful at a time when people washed their hair once a week at most. It meant that when you got up in the morning you could stop your hair sticking up all over the place by slapping a handful of pomade on. As we had none my mother spent ten minutes applying spit to my head.

It might seem odd to people who have never worked in service because you would think that the butler would have known all about me. I'd always lived on the estate and had worked in the house and garden for ten years and more already. But I think it was important to spruce myself up as a sign of respect to the butler and also because he needed to see how I would look dressed up. Being a footman was almost all about how you looked in a suit.

I set off across the fields to the house and at the old entrance where I'd gone in every day as hall boy I met the maid who'd thrown a bucket of water over me and the cook who used to belt me as I ran past. I think they had both mellowed a bit or perhaps they thought I wasn't such a bad lot after all because they smiled at me and said 'Good luck'. I crossed the kitchen and went up the corridor and the stairs to the heavy door that led into the butler's rooms.

I knocked and heard nothing. I waited for a short while. As the corridor was dark and I worried I would not be seen, I leaned to one side and peeped through the small window that looked into the butler's room just to the side of the door. I was horrified to discover that as I looked Mr Carter was already staring at the window and right into my eyes. I jumped back and waited, mortified that I'd been caught and getting redder in the face by the second.

After another twenty seconds I heard a voice: 'Come in.'

I opened the door and there was Mr Carter behind his desk and immaculately dressed in a black suit of the old-fashioned kind. I mean he wore a frock coat and a beautifully starched butterfly collar and waist-coat.

'Mr Sharpe?' he asked.

'Yes sir – Mr Carter, I mean.'

'You've just learned your first lesson,' he said.

I must have seemed a complete fool to him because I hadn't a clue what he was on about. I just shifted uneasily and stared at the papers on his desk. My face I think was crimson by now and under the unfamiliar suit the sweat trickled down my back.

'Do you get my meaning?' he asked.

'I'm afraid not, sir,' I replied, forgetting again that I should have called him Mr Carter.

'You mustn't call me sir,' he said, but in a more gentle tone. 'I'm Mr Carter.'

'Yes sir, I mean Mr Carter.'

'It's always difficult,' he said, 'because we are all naturally curious and impatient, especially when we are young. In service we have to learn to show no curiosity or impatience at all so far as our superiors are concerned. Our job is to be available when we are needed, to speak when spoken to. But at the same time we do need to make sure we are at hand. What you should have done was to knock more loudly and then waited without curiosity, without looking to see if you had been heard, confident that your presence had been noted. James will show you your duties.'

He waved towards the door and that was that. My interview, if that's what it can be called, was over.

Now, Mr Carter seemed cold and hard to me, but it was all an act as I soon discovered from the senior footman, James. I owe a lot to Mr Carter because to a very large extent I modelled my behaviour on his and he was a formidable presence. Legend in the house had it that he never put a foot wrong, never smiled, never moved at more than a stately pace along the corridors and up the stairs and never spoke out of turn, dropped or broke anything or even raised his voice. He was a legend among butlers.

At the very moment Mr Carter had waved me out, James was ready waiting on the other side of the door. It was as if he'd appeared out of nowhere. That was typical of the smooth way Mr Carter ran things.

'If you want to get to the top, copy Carter.' That was almost the first thing James told me as we went off together for a twenty-minute chat after I had been dismissed by Mr Carter.

James, the first footman, was a lovely man. He was

tall as all footmen were, with a narrow face and surprisingly good teeth – I say surprisingly because most of us didn't see a dentist from one year's end to the next. James had unusual green eyes too and thin, light brown hair of which he was very proud, although his hair was so wispy he almost looked prematurely bald. But James's most noticeable feature was a terrible stutter.

When I'd seen him around occasionally when I was hall boy he had behaved as if I was invisible but we got along really well from the first moment we worked together. Although, 'You *were* invisible,' he said to me once. 'All hall boys are invisible!'

It was only when I became junior footman that I found out about his stammer. Now, you might think a stammer would be a terrible problem for a footman who wanted to become a butler. Not a bit of it. When he said, 'Yes sir,' or 'Yes madam,' or 'Very good, m'lord,' there was no hint of a problem and since he only ever said these two or three stock phrases to his employers they were probably not even aware that he stammered. Then I discovered that even if he did very occasionally have to get out a longer sentence to a member of the family he still showed no sign of a stammer.

When I got to know him well I asked him about this. 'I don't stammer with them upstairs because it would be like showing the enemy you were afraid in a war. I stammer with my friends, not with that lot.' He was quite an eccentric. One of the things I loved about

James was that he always made jokes about his stammer when we were in the pub or anywhere else away from work. He'd get a few sentences out and then it was as if he had remembered he had a problem and he would just stop in his tracks, but he had a brilliantly funny way of getting going again.

This is how it would go. He'd say, 'I was just getting along by the hedge and this bloody car came along really fa ... fa ... fa ... fa ... oh fuck it!' Or he'd say, 'Thank God posh people don't have fer, fer, fer, fer, fer fucking fish knives!'

He loved swearing partly I think because he had to be so controlled, as we all did, during working hours. When he had a few hours off and could get down to the pub it was his chance to release the safety valve. That was another of his favourite phrases. He also used to say, 'Think about it, Bob. If I tried to swear deliberately I couldn't do it, could I? I couldn't tell someone to 'eff off to save my life because I'd get to the F and get fer ... fer ... fer ... fer ... fucking stuck.'

But James thought the world of Mr Carter. He said, 'Carter has the magic and I'm getting as much of it as I can as quick as I can.' He meant that he wanted to model himself on Carter so that he could apply for a butler's job as soon as possible. Butlers were the best paid of all domestic servants and so elevated in their own and everyone else's estimation that they seemed almost as good as the highest members of any family in the land. Of course they weren't really but to other servants lower down the butler was God. And James was right about copying Mr Carter. You had to have a certain air of seriousness and aloofness to be a really good butler even if it was all just an act. What really made us young men want to be butlers were the tips – butlers' tips were legendary. You heard about people earning double their wages in a year through tips alone. But as I later discovered sometimes they expected a lot more than butlering in return for those tips.

James's real name was Reg but in the best houses back then all footmen were called either John or James. So from now on my work name was John. I have no idea where this nonsense started and it may not have been universal but it was the general rule in the houses I worked in. I think it may have got round the problem that footmen did look the part, in that they were tall and good-looking, but then they had what were seen by their employers as lower-class names – like Bob and Reg.

Also, having a work name added to your sense that you had to be another person during working hours if you wanted to get anywhere. This is why you'll notice when you talk to a retired servant, especially a male servant who worked his way up to butler, that they have a sort of halfway accent. If you listen carefully you can still hear the country accent or the London accent they grew up with but there is only a trace of it left because they couldn't help but gradually copy the people they worked for. If you worked for his lordship you couldn't say, 'I never done it,' or 'I ain't done nothing,' which you might have grown up saying. No, you quickly learned to say 'I didn't do it,' and 'I haven't done anything.' And all butlers learned to pronounce their tees and their aitches!

Some butlers I knew felt they had risen in the world – socially risen that is – because they saw themselves as able to speak properly and they'd learned about dressing, serving wine, silver and pictures and that sort of thing. But the sad fact is that all their efforts to ape their superiors simply confirmed their status as servants. They couldn't win, you see. If you didn't speak as well as you could, if you didn't try to leave your accent behind, you didn't get on; but the better you spoke the more your employer was aware that you were just aping your betters. Sometimes they mocked you for it. It all depended on whether you had a kind boss – and there were some of those around I will admit – or a haughty old bastard who liked to humiliate you. And there were a lot of those around too.

I remember on one occasion soon after I'd been allowed to wait at table, standing at the wall with James while the butler went round with the wine. I didn't normally listen to the table conversation – you'd be amazed how you learn to drift off – but this time I gradually became aware that they were talking about us, the servants in the room I mean. The butler and two footmen.

The family and their guests seated round the table had had plenty to drink which might explain it, but I was amazed to hear James and John discussed as if they were miles away.

His lordship said, 'John is a good fellow, but that is as far as it goes. Whatever these socialists and Bolsheviks say, the fact remains that no amount of education can erase the nature of one's birth. This is something the modern world will come to understand. The old families have lasted not because of education or money but because of breeding and John, James and the others, delightful though they are, would not be happy in any higher sphere. They would be out of their depth. They would feel inadequate to the situation. It is a simple fact.'

And on they went all agreeing with each other that poor old John – not even using my real name – was no better than an intelligent ape. They also said some terrible things about Jews and black people which were perfectly routine back then.

'I don't like London at all now,' said his lordship once. 'Too many niggers.'

One of his daughters had danced with a young man at a ball in London in my second or third year as a footman and for months afterwards I heard her father return again and again with horror to the fact that the man she had danced with looked no better than 'a dirty little Jew'.

That was the phrase he used. Of course I was no better than the rest of them and at the time thought nothing of this. In fact I probably agreed with it. We were all prejudiced because we grew up in a world where we thought English people were superior to everyone – even English servants thought they were superior to the best from any other country.

People used the word Jewish to mean tight-fisted. So you'd say, 'He's a bit Jewish,' meaning he was close with his money; and there would have been people who used the phrase who had no idea that Jewish meant anything else. But other people got it in the neck too. If something didn't work well or was awkward to use – a kettle or whatever – people would routinely say, 'Oh, this is a bit Irish.'

At the time I wasn't bothered by the fact that they talked about me at that dinner. I accepted that, in their eyes, I was a lesser sort. I just shrugged it off when they were rude about me. We lived in their cottages and houses and ate the food they paid for and took the wages they paid so if they wanted to be rude to us, well, that was up to them. But I often wondered if the angels were looking down what they would make of it all.

Chapter 11

My only real concern for my first six months as a footman was not to make too many mistakes and to learn from James. I asked him endless questions and watched him at work. He had learned by copying Mr Carter; I learned by copying him. It was the way you handled a new job in those days. Like an apprenticeship. As hall boy I had been there only to work for the other servants. As footman it was very different. I had to listen out for the bells that said that someone upstairs wanted something. All the bells were on a rack in the servants' hall and a complicated system of wires made them ring if a cord was pulled upstairs. I'd note the room name – the sitting or dining room – and set off up the stairs. When you arrived a member of the family might say, 'I'm cold, John. Do something with the fire, would you.' The old lady would never say, 'Rake up the fire, John,' or 'Give it a good poke,' or even 'Put a few more logs on the fire, John.' I asked James about this. 'Why doesn't she say exactly what she wants?'

'Well it's like this,' said James. 'If she said exactly what she wanted it might indicate to you that she understands how fires work or what needs to be done to make them work; but when you are well-to-do you really want to suggest to people – especially the servants – that you have no idea how a fire works or what needs to be done to make it work. If you did let slip that you know about fires people might think you were less upper class than you want them to think.'

I thought James was joking but as the years passed I had so many examples of people implying they knew nothing about the most basic things that I knew he must be right. There was a sort of code. Take writing paper – it was always called writing paper and never notepaper. Notepaper was dreadfully common, can you believe!

So her ladyship would sit on her sofa (never a settee), ring the bell and wait for me to come up three floors. She'd then say to me, 'John, bring me some writing paper.' The desk was six feet from the sofa and I'd come up three floors to get the paper for her. It was like the old Oscar Wilde joke where one character says to another, 'I call a spade a spade,' and the other replies, 'I'm very glad to say that I have never seen a spade.'

In most cases if her ladyship's bell rang I told James and he attended to it. The junior footman didn't do the principal members of the family unless the senior footman was unavailable. I could do for visitors and younger members of the family. Mr Carter only really got into action at dinner. The rest of his time was spent looking after the silver and keeping the rest of the servants at their work or helping his lordship.

We had a phone in the house but I was told never to answer it. Only the first footman or the butler could pick it up. But since hardly anyone else round about had a phone I don't remember it ringing often. And it was so newfangled anyway that everyone was slightly afraid of it.

As junior footman I had to learn to set out the breakfast things in the dining room early each morning. Mostly James helped me but Mr Carter would always appear from nowhere just to check that everything was going smoothly. He was absolutely precise about everything and would move a plate or a dish an inch this way or an inch that way until he thought it was all just right. That was the thing about butlers, and I took it to heart early on: they had to make sure their staff ran the house like clockwork. This meant that if the staff were up to the mark the butler could while away much of the day staring out the window in his pantry. Everything had to be done precisely as it had always been done. People hated change then far more than they did later. And if a member of the family complained about something the butler couldn't say, 'Oh that's the footman's fault,' because he, the butler, was responsible for the footman.

Setting out the breakfast things in a big house isn't as easy as it sounds. The first footman carried up the silver while I carried up the china – again, you see, hierarchy. Only the first footman or the butler could carry the silver. The best table stuff was handled by the first footman, and when guests were staying there was a ton of stuff to shift up- and downstairs each and every day.

We worked our way round the table putting everything in position and knowing that the butler would check every bit of work after we'd done it. I hadn't a clue what I was doing at first but James was a good teacher. He was expert and would place the knives and forks and plates – as well as the dishes on the sideboard – with military precision. Everything had to be in its right place with decorative silver in the centre of the table, certain kinds of flowers at certain times of year, a thick linen tablecloth, endless spoons and plates and napkins all of the highest quality. At the outset it was bewildering.

'Whatever you do don't break any of the bloody china or you'll be in very hot water,' said James. 'It all matches and there is a lot of it and they won't be happy to have to get a replacement piece. They'll dock it from your wages and you'll be marked down as a butterfingers and not butler material. You can't afford to make a single mistake.' James was right. All butlers prided themselves on never making a mistake and never dropping a thing. The level of concentration required was exhausting at first. No wonder butlers had a reputation for drinking when they had a bit of time off.

*   *   *

From the start of my time as a footman I did it as if my life depended on it. I had somehow gone from hardly thinking about my future to being very ambitious. It was James's influence I think. The structure of the servants' world tended to make you ambitious – either that or you left and did something else. If your heart wasn't in it you couldn't really do the job well enough and then you would make mistakes.

But for all our work and for all the fact that we were talked about and talked down to there were compensations. We observed the antics of the family as much as they made sure we were kept under surveillance. And what a family it was!

The most extraordinary thing about them en masse was the number of children in the family and the fact that they all looked and sounded exactly alike. They were all grown up at this time – probably in their late twenties, thirties and perhaps even forties. There must have been a dozen or more and I can remember standing at the edge of the dining table and handing the sauces and gravies round while Carter dealt with the wine, thinking, 'I have no idea which son or daughter is which or how many there are.' And do you know I never really got the hang of it because you never saw the whole lot sitting down together or staying in the house at the same time.

The sons and daughters turned up to visit in ones and twos for an odd night or they might stay a few days or more, but the exact individual and whether he or she was the same as the one who was there the night before was always impossible to determine. They all looked exactly alike.

Dinner upstairs always lasted at least two or three hours and it was much harder to determine who exactly we were dealing with. There might be eight or nine sons and daughters round the table. They got up and wandered off halfway through the soup or the main course only to come back ten minutes later or not return at all. Or just one would come back, or three. Now and then two of them would get into an argument and get up and go out and then it was impossible to tell when another one came back whether it was one of the ones who had just gone out. Not only did they all look alike and dress alike – they all sounded alike too!

I remember clearly the extraordinary way they spoke to each other. It seemed to me to be completely batty. Their conversation would go something like this:

'Cedric you really are a beast,'

'But Emily I tell you the bloody man wore a green suit.'

'Impossible. Simply impossible. I don't believe it. No one would speak to him. He would be utterly abandoned.'

'Well, I might tell you we had fits of giggleswick. We shrieked.'

'I should think you would.'

'He will be marooned. How dreadful.'

And on and on they would go like this for the whole

two hours it took to go from the first course to the fifth. Sometimes they'd carry on when the brother or sister they had been talking to had got up and left the room. The fact is that they hardly needed a listener. They'd have talked to the furniture if need be.

Meanwhile I would interrupt now and then with a sauce or to take a plate and the conversation would take another turn.

I had to wear a dress suit with tails and a waistcoat and ridiculous big brass buttons – they seemed horribly oversized to me – but by the end of my career all footmen and butlers were wearing an ordinary suit, what came to be called a lounge suit, a term I have always hated.

All went well with this footman business for the first few years. After an initial feeling that I'd never get the hang of it – it was so different in some respects from the work of hall boy or garden boy – I gradually began to feel that it wasn't that difficult after all. But there were some very odd incidents that reminded me how strange the relationship between master and servant could be.

Chapter 12

It all began one autumn when they had a dozen or more guests staying from Friday to Monday. The upper classes in those days never referred to staying for a weekend because that might imply they had to be at work on Monday and that would never do. It was the middle classes who stayed with each other for weekends.

I had been told I had to valet for one of the younger guests. He was part of a group that had come for the shooting. I believe he was a friend of the youngest son but his lordship's friends were also part of the group. My man didn't have his own valet and, as Mr Carter explained, it was the junior footman who became temporary valet under these circumstances. If the man had been a good bit older or titled then James would have done the valeting. But in practice all older men had their own valets so the problem very rarely arose.

I had a quick course of instruction in valeting before the young man arrived. James put me right on several things including ironing shirts, unpacking bags and hanging clothes in the wardrobe. The key was to be very, very tidy and very methodical. I was to carry up a tray with tea and biscuits and then hot water for the young man's morning bath and to lay out his bath things and razor, his hairbrushes and combs and his shirts and collars, his suit and shoes, making sure all were clean and nicely folded. Of course when a visitor had just arrived you could usually be sure that his clothing would have been packed by a servant at home so it was likely to be clean and well folded already, usually immaculately so, and often interleaved with fine sheets of white tissue paper.

Well, this young man I'd been given – Mr David – had a suitcase that was very different from the norm. Where I'd expected beautifully folded shirts and socks, drawers and trousers, I found sticky medicine bottles, a half-empty bottle of whisky and an enormous mangled jumble of filthy clothes. The suitcase itself was a beautiful thing about three and a half feet long and two feet deep, solid leather, and I could hardly lift it. I had found the suitcase thrown on the bed when I went up to make sure everything was ready. Of the young man himself there was as yet no sign.

When guests arrived their servants brought the luggage in or if they arrived without servants we were sent out to get it. Their suitcases were emptied while they went to the drawing room and had drinks or sat about talking. But this time it was very different. All I could do was look at the mess I had to deal with, thinking, 'Oh my God what do I do now?' I'd only known what to do if everything had been tidy and neat as James told me it would be. This pile of dirty washing left me momentarily flummoxed. What bad luck to get someone like this on my first valeting duty!

As it turned out it was my first really positive experience as a servant with the sole exception of my time with poor old Kent.

After standing looking perplexed for what was probably only a minute but felt like an hour I heard a voice weakly saying, 'Hello.'

I said hello back. Then the voice came again.

'Would you mind helping me up? I'm afraid I'm rather stuck.'

The voice seemed to be coming from the other side of the big bed, which was well away from the door near which I had been standing. I cautiously peered round the bottom end of the bed and there on the floor wearing only his underthings was a thin young man who was clearly very drunk. As I helped him up I noticed he was rather odd-looking. He had a slightly scrunched-up face – too much inbreeding said James when I told him later – and tiny grey eyes that really were too close together. His rather long hair was prematurely grey in places and grew an amazingly long way down on his forehead. But unlike anyone else I'd encountered among the upper classes he seemed completely natural and unaffected and spoke to me as if he'd known me a long time and there really

wasn't much difference between us at all. It astonished me – until I remembered he was drunk.

'Thank heavens you've arrived. Just in time to
prevent a serious collision.' He leaned against me
while he spoke and absolutely stank of whisky.

'Sorry, had a little too much firewater. Terribly
sorry about breathing all over you. Could you just put
me on the bed, which is where I was trying to go when
I fell. Thanks. Very good of you.'

I eased him on to the end of the bed where he
flopped down and groaned loudly.

'Terrible imposition,' he said, 'but would you mind
sorting out my clothes. They could do with a bit of a
wash and iron if there's a laundry here.'

With that he sat upright, pulled off his vest and
long underpants, handed them to me and then fell
back down on the bed completely naked. Within
seconds he was fast asleep.

I took all the messed-up dirty things from his suitcase and went downstairs as quickly as I could to see
James.

'He sounds a bit of a character,' he said when I
explained the problem. 'You get the odd one like that.
Mind he doesn't try to f . . . f . . . f . . . fucking seduce
you!'

James never teased me normally and I assumed this
was teasing, but when I said so he said he wasn't
joking at all.

'Oh these upper-class people, they're not like us,'
he said. 'They'll sleep with their wives, their wives'

sisters, their best friend's dog, the servants, the servants' dogs. Animal, vegetable or mineral they'll sleep with it. It's all to do with having nothing to do all day and of course their public schools. I'm not kidding. Everyone at public schools buggers everyone else. It's part of the curriculum.'

I laughed at this but was slightly shocked too. I had hardly been more than fifteen miles from the estate in my life and hadn't a clue about homosexuality. James, by contrast, seemed to know about everything and delighted in telling me the most outrageous *facts* which he always insisted really were facts. I usually didn't believe a word he said but as I grew older I realised that in many ways he really did know what he was talking about.

Sex was a big thing in country houses where most of the occupants and those who visited them had very little else to do. Even as a hall boy I'd heard the servants occasionally talking about the goings-on upstairs. Usually it was the cook telling the maids off for gossiping about things they'd seen and heard, but when I became a footman I quickly realised that sex was central to the lives of the upper classes, although to give them their due they were very discreet about what went on.

That young man I valeted for was slightly less than discreet. After he woke up on the morning I rescued him from the floor he rang his bell just before lunch. James nodded at me and said, 'Off you go, but watch your step. Tell him you want to be paid first!'

I smiled at that but was a little uncomfortable. I

was one of those innocents who thought sex something you only did to have children and you didn't do
it till you were married and that men certainly didn't
have sex with other men.

When I arrived back in the young man's rooms he
smiled at me and apologised for dragging me all the
way back up the stairs. He was in some very thick,
very fusty pyjamas.

'I'd also like to apologise for my disgraceful behaviour earlier on. Completely drunk at ten in the
morning. Absolutely disgraceful. Do you drink?'

I said I had a few pints with my brother now and then.

'Is that all? How very good you are. But we can't
have that. What's the local pub like by the way? I
might have to try it.'

The upper classes were good at this sort of conversation. Talking about nonsense but in an entertaining
and offhand way. Working-class people like me could
never do it. And my replies would have confirmed his
view that the lower orders were just stupid.

'I'm afraid it's just an ordinary pub, sir.'

'Good,' he said. 'That's how I like them.' And he
winked at me.

'We might go and have a pint some day.'

'Yes, sir,' I said, but thinking, 'This one is completely
mad.'

'Look,' he said, 'I've borrowed a suit from my friend
– he's the only one I know in the house really – would
you mind polishing my shoes while I get dressed?'

*   *   *

So I picked up his shoes, said yes sir and took off downstairs. His clothes had been washed and ironed below stairs but they were still drying and wouldn't be ready until the next day, although none of this seemed to bother him. He'd borrowed a suit of clothes and that was it. No embarrassment at all. By the time I got his shoes back to him he was fully dressed and with his hair smoothed down. He was also singing at the top of his voice.

'I'm off to be bored to death now,' he said before smiling and leaving the room. And later when he winked at me during dinner I began to be convinced that he wanted to be my friend, which was nonsense of course. He was the same with everyone. At dinner he kept up an amusing but completely irrelevant stream of light-hearted banter and was clearly a favourite with the family. They treated him slightly as if he was the court jester, which, I suppose, in a way he was.

He said, 'Do you know, my father thinks that riding should be recommended for what he calls pansies and Bolsheviks. When I asked him about this I discovered that he was being perfectly serious. I told him I thought it was a splendid idea and that he should write immediately to *The Times* and to the government.'

And so it went on right through dinner while I stood like a waxwork in the shadows at the edge of the room gazing out across the diners. And I was most impressed that he seemed to know who was who among the numerous adult sons and daughters who, as usual, drifted in and out as the evening wore on.

I have to say I wasn't even put out when having run him a bath the next morning he asked me to hold his towel and help him out of the water. He then leaned on me and asked me to help him to a chair. 'Hot water makes one rather faint,' he said. He also asked for a drink.

Two days later he rang his bell and I went up to his room. Without a word he handed me a ten-shilling tip which was very good of him. I reckon I was earning about £40 a year at this time so it was as if Christmas had come early. But then he said, 'Awfully nice to have met you. And by the way, would you get rid of this?' He handed me a set of false teeth in a glass of water.

James said, 'He should have paid you a sight more than ten bob for making you hang around while he was having his bath. He wanted to show you what he looked like in the f . . . f . . . f . . . fucking flesh!'

James might have been right but I had my ten shillings and no harm done and at least the young man hadn't talked to me as if I was something he had trodden in!

Chapter 13

I was junior footman until I was nearly thirty but young Mr David was the oddest person I encountered above stairs during all that time. Below stairs *everyone* seemed odd to me – even Mr Carter, stern and serious figure though he was, had his eccentricities.

James told me that when they cleaned the silver together they used gin to bring up the shine. But Mr Carter didn't just clean with gin. He would continually be taking sips of it from the bottle. He didn't mind a bit if James noticed. James swore that Mr Carter used to pour a bit on his hands too and then smooth it through his hair. And if he spilled something on his trousers he would immediately tip a bit of gin on to the mark and swear it was the best thing for getting out stains. I didn't believe all this but Mr Carter certainly always smelled slightly of gin and I was amazed the family didn't complain, but perhaps that was because they too were all heavy drinkers who started on the gin very early every morning.

Other servants had their odd habits too.

One of the housemaids, who was called Lottie, used to cry quietly almost all the time. I felt aghast that anyone could be so unhappy. She blew her nose and wiped her eyes continually on the duster she used to clean upstairs. Eventually another housemaid told me she wasn't sad at all but had a medical problem that made her sneeze and made her eyes water – it was probably just hay fever but I never heard the words hay fever until the 1960s. Lottie must have smeared gallons of saliva and mucous all over the family furniture and mirrors, sneezing and blowing on them for twenty years!

Chapter 14

My father, always a bit of a cold, distant figure as many fathers were then, had grown more remote in the time I worked in the house because we hardly saw each other. I hadn't lived at home since becoming a footman and I had the feeling my father thought I was getting a bit above myself. He never mentioned anything specific but I suspect he noticed that my speech had gradually changed, as it had under relentless pressure from Mr Carter and James. They corrected my country accent whenever I said something it was felt would not go down well with the family. I think these changes drew me gradually away from my own family. I still saw my mother who was delighted at how I was getting on at the house, but she was always uncomfortable on the few occasions when my father came in. The world of servants could be very divisive because it was so hierarchical. I was sad at the gulf that was opening up but had no idea how to do anything about it. Then came an enormous and sudden change.

My father died. My mother said he had been sitting up in bed one night when she came up to join him. He was perfectly well and had been talking about clearing the gutters of leaves and getting a new dog. He stopped talking for a moment, let out a small moan and then tipped sideways. My mother reached him just in time to stop him falling right out of his bed. It was either a heart attack or a stroke but as he died instantly no one bothered much to find out the details. What was the point of knowing exactly what killed him? The doctor issued the death certificate and just a few friends from the village and from among the local keepers came the night before he was buried. The body lay in its coffin on the kitchen table with his old waxy face glimmering in the candlelight. When I looked at my father in his coffin the thing that I remember is how shrunken he seemed. To me he had always seemed a giant who could lift anything and work sixteen-hour days in freezing weather or blistering heat. Now he was a little yellow thing in a box. I also looked round the house to see if there was anything of his I could keep to remind me of him. But there was nothing. Apart from his clothes and his gun and pipe he had nothing at all, which seemed a sad thing to me after he'd lived so long. And then he was gone.

It's always easier in the short term to cope with the death of a parent if you have not been close, but in the long run that lack of closeness makes the death harder to bear. By the time I myself was old I thought about my father more often and brooded over how fifty years earlier I might have made things better, or he might have, or at least I might have said something to him. But there we are; there are many things we can't change and that was one of them and we were all very good at avoiding saying anything about how we felt back then.

I was allowed a week off – a rare thing then – to help my mother but she shooed me back to work after a few days saying that it was better if we all had something to occupy ourselves with. She was lucky, too, as the estate let her stay in the house as my brothers were still keepering there and living at home.

My father's death, despite our lack of closeness, began the process of cutting me free from the estate. That and all the stories I'd heard from James about life on other estates and especially life in London houses which he painted with a very vivid brush.

'What do we do here, except go to the pub when we have some time off?' he used to ask me. 'In London it's different. On your evening off you might meet fifty girls.'

That seemed a great temptation indeed. We both decided to look for jobs in the city and began answering advertisements in the local newspaper. I found a few situations for second footman in various houses and these jobs paid a bit more than I was getting – in one case a lot more. I carefully wrote out my letters of application and proudly showed them to James before sending them. He said he thought my handwriting alone would do the trick but he also explained that he himself hadn't yet found anything he quite liked the look of.

'You'll have to hurry up or I will be there before you,' I said.

'Don't you worry I'll soon find the best job there is for first footman in a really big establishment and then we'll meet regularly and try all the pubs – and the girls.'

By the time I'd had a reply to one of my letters asking me to go for an interview I had a feeling that James was not serious about leaving at all, or rather that he was serious but that he wouldn't ultimately be able to do it. He never sounded quite convincing when he enthused about the big city and all it had to offer. And I was right. He never did take a job away from the estate. There was always a good reason of course. The job was in the wrong part of London. He didn't like the sound of the set-up. It was the wrong time of year. Every time I wrote to him once I'd moved he was always planning to get going but somehow he never did. In the end I stopped asking him and our letters eventually dried up. He spent the rest of his working life on the estate I think, but without his enthusiasm I might never have moved on so I was always grateful to him.

Chapter 15

It was 1930. The Great War had become an embarrassment, something no one wanted to talk about. Looking back I feel a little guilty that we cared so little about the carnage that had gone on so recently, but it was a time when people felt they should look forward not back. There was no nostalgia for the past as there was to be later, except perhaps among a few elderly aristocrats who lamented the loss of the cosy world that been shattered by the war and taxes. I remember hearing my employers complaining bitterly that their investments should be taxed at all. It was fine for working people to pay taxes but not the rich. Extraordinary, isn't it, that they felt that was fair. The argument they used was that they had a position to keep up.

The 1920s had famously been the years of the Bright Young Things who kicked over the traces and did as they pleased. Of course this had little effect on us the servants except that a subtle change crept over the way everyone – even servants – spoke and thought. A lot of hidebound views began to disappear and while the children of the rich danced and drank and smoked cigarettes to the horror of their Victorian parents, we began to think more of ourselves. There was a feeling in the air that if you didn't like a job you could just hop it in a way that had not really been possible before. There was a feeling that however grand your employer, he or she no longer had the power of life and death over you. It was the difference between my father and me. He would have thought I was mad if I suggested he change jobs whereas I wanted to get on and didn't mind moving in the least if that was likely to help me.

I remember the elation I felt when finally I was offered a job as second footman. It was in a large house in Regent's Park in central London owned by an elderly woman known to everyone as the Dowager. She was grand and extremely wealthy but I'm not sure she was quite as grand as she liked to make out. She also had very strange ideas about what a footman should do.

I arrived at the house on the morning of my interview having taken a train to London and then a cab from the station. I was full of excitement. London back then was the place people talked about all the time, because there was no romance to living in the country when you were poor. My brother Billy used to say, 'The only thing you can do on a wet night round here in January is cut your throat – or someone else's!' London was shops and dances, plays and girls. The countryside was nobody about, trees dripping rain and miles to walk across the fields to the nearest shop or pub and always the same pub and the same shop. And you never met a soul you didn't know which meant that if you so much as looked at a village girl half the county knew about it before the day was out. London meant a sort of freedom.

I must be one of the last people alive who has travelled by hansom cab. There were still a few in London in the 1920s and even the early 1930s. A lot of older people didn't trust the new motor cars and a few of the old cabbies hated the new motor cabs and couldn't learn to drive them. Rather than risk walking and getting lost I thought I'd waste a shilling and get a cab to take me from the station straight to the house. I was also feeling well set up and confident that my time had arrived, so I thought why not – take a cab, it's what a gentleman would do!

If you weren't used to it getting into a hansom was a bit of a rigmarole. You climbed in through the front rather than through a door at the side, which is where other carriages had their doors. The passenger part of the hansom was very low down while the cabby's seat was six feet up in the air behind the cab. Here the driver sat exposed to all weathers. In most carriages of course the driver sat in front of the passengers and immediately behind the horse or horses. Not so in a hansom. The reins went from the driver up at the back over the top of the cab in which the passenger sat and then down to the horse. This gave the passenger a prime view of the horse's arse, as the first footman in my new house said when he heard I'd taken a hansom. It also kept the driver out of sight and out of mind and in his rightful place at the rear.

I was amazed at how nippy that cab was. It dodged and turned like an ice skater in and out of the motor buses, lorries and carts that packed the roads. That was why the hansom had been so popular. Because of that low centre of gravity it could turn very quickly without tipping up. Even now I remember the smell of the old black crinkled leatherwork, and on the floor there was a bit of straw to absorb the rainwater and help keep the passengers' feet warm and dry.

Anyway, the old driver knew from my clothes I was not very likely to be a visitor to the house so without a word he nodded and took me straight to the back of the house. This was down an alleyway rather like a narrow mews. Like most cabbies he knew all the big houses within a mile or so of the main London stations. He would have made a good living by ferrying the rich from their central London houses in Mayfair, Kensington and Regent's Park to the great railway stations. At this time no one would have thought of going any distance into the countryside by motor car. With no major roads and slow cars it would have taken forever. No, the railway was still king.

I hopped out of the hansom and paid the cabby, who tipped his hat and lurched off down the road without a word. I knocked at the large black door and waited. A tiny maid opened it for me and stood aside. I stepped into a long narrow hall and realised – not for the last time – how similar the servants' parts of all big houses were. It was as if the owners of these houses had got together and decided that anything brighter than dull greys and madhouse green would cause a revolution among the lower orders.

'Would you mind waiting here?' said the sparrow-sized maid as she closed the door.

In my most serious voice I replied, 'Not a bit.' I must admit I didn't want her to think I was a nobody so I was quite snooty in my tone, although of course she'd have known I was a nobody really!

I sat on a long and very hard hall bench which was of an unusual design and one you never see these days. It was about twelve feet long or more. The backrest was hinged. It could be flipped so that it was first at one side of the bench and then at the other. This was very useful because it meant the whole thing could be moved across the hall without all the bother of taking it outside, turning it round and then bringing it back in. It was rather like the seats you found on trams at that time. At the terminus the tram conductor would walk through his tram flipping all the backs of the seats so that the passengers would be facing forward on the return journey even though the tram itself had simply gone into reverse.

The other thing I noticed was a massive old tavern clock with a black lacquered case and faded gold lettering, nailed high up on the far end wall. All I could make out then and later was the word 'Fear', which might have been the remains of the name of the maker – but it made me wonder if it wasn't a warning about what I should expect. I discovered that it was one of about sixty clocks in the house and that the Dowager employed a full-time clock winder and repairer to keep them accurate. She was a stickler for punctuality.

The clock was just about the only thing to look at in that hall so I was left twiddling my thumbs for a few minutes until a very grand and immensely tall person turned the corner and lunged towards me. This was George the first footman, a man I was to get to know well. He was a very grave character. He looked me up and down and said, 'You'll probably do.' He jerked his head back the way he'd come and set off. I galloped after him as best I could through what seemed a maze of tunnels and passages – all green and grey of course and badly lit by gas. We reached the sort of huge door that looked as if it would take five men to open.

The ceiling had gradually become taller with each change of direction as we'd raced along – George never went at anything less than breakneck speed – and where we finally stopped I reckoned the ceiling must have been twelve feet up. Nevertheless the door in front of us, which was at least four and a half feet wide, went right up to the ceiling. It had two small glass panels at the top to admit a bit of light to the hall and six giant hinges.

George rapped fiercely on the door, pushed it open a fraction and stuck his head in.

'Sharpe,' he said, pulled his head out without waiting for an answer, and shut the door. He turned to look at me, nodded again and stalked off like a heron. I say stalked because George was the tallest footman I ever encountered. He made James, who was well over six feet, look like a dwarf. He was also one of the most remarkable and eccentric characters I ever met and I can tell you that in the butlering and footman line you met a lot of eccentrics. George's eccentricities were well matched in that house by only one person – the Dowager herself.

I was left standing by that huge door for a few moments longer and then it slowly opened and a hand appeared, took my arm and pulled me in.

Here was the man I had come to see: the butler. In those days all the male staff in a house were appointed by the butler, and although the housekeeper appointed the cook and the maids she was also ultimately responsible to the butler.

The first thing that surprised me about Mr Chapman, the Dowager's butler, was that he looked quite short – which was a rare thing in a butler. This was partly due to his being very overweight. I suspect he was getting on for five feet ten or eleven in reality; but it didn't help that he was always standing next to George. George later told me Mr Chapman had only put the weight on since becoming butler. 'That man can't keep his hands off the pies,' he said, 'and if there are no pies to get hold of he gets hold of the cook instead.'

The first time I set eyes on him Mr Chapman was wearing a dark suit with a tie so fiercely knotted that it looked as if it was cutting off his air supply and making his face very red and round in the process. He gazed intently at me over the top of his round blue-lensed spectacles and said nothing. Then he gave me a huge smile and said:

'What are we here for, Mr Sharpe?'

I was momentarily baffled as the only other person I'd ever heard ask this sort of question was the priest.

'To work?' I suggested.

'No, no, no, Mr Sharpe,' said Mr Chapman. 'We are here to serve. Stand over there please.'

He indicated a place near the door and against the wall. He then opened the twelve-foot door and ushered George in. George was carrying a small pair of what looked like callipers. He knelt down next to me, squeezed my calf through my trousers and applied the callipers.

Mr Chapman said: 'The Dowager likes a good leg for ceremonial occasions. What's the news, George?'

'He'll do,' said George. He then turned and left the room.

This was all happening at high speed so I had almost no time to be astonished – but astonished I was. For some reason George had given my leg a really hard squeeze and it bloody hurt. I was desperate to crouch down and rub the pain away but didn't dare with Mr Chapman pacing the room.

'Start at the end of the month if you can,' he said. 'If not, the end of the following month. Good day.'

And that was the end of my interview. George was waiting for me and, round-shouldered and leaning forward, he led me back down the corridors towards the back door. Here he seemed almost to have to stoop to fit himself under the low ceiling.

'I put in a good word for you,' he said. I couldn't understand that at all as I'd never met him till that day and I never did really find out what he meant. At least a third of all the things he said to me over the coming year were equally baffling.

I went out the door and was turning to say goodbye when George said,

'Half a tick. I'll come with you.'

With that he pulled on his own coat and fell into step next to me.

I had planned to walk back to the station to save money and I explained this to George who said, 'Good man. I'll show you the way.'

We soon reached a road that ran along by the side of Regent's Park and George pulled out a bundle wrapped in newspaper he'd been carrying under his arm – it looked like he'd bought fish and chips for the whole family. As we went along he looked over his shoulder twice and then hurled the package over the fence and into the park without a word. He then marched along talking all the time but everything he said seemed like nonsense as far as I could understand it. I can't remember much of it but it centred on people he knew I was unlikely ever to have heard of. He said, 'As you will recall I told Pat that it was just not on. I had no intention of being mucked about after what happened when we were at the Grapes.' I had no idea how to respond to anything he said so I said nothing. This didn't seem to bother him a bit.

I followed his rapid gangling form as best I could, and then without altering his pace he dodged down a side road and into a dark little pub. 'It's called the Footman's Rest,' he said. 'You don't want to miss it. All part of the job.'

The pub wasn't called the Footman's Rest at all but that's what George called it.

Once inside the little bar he was completely at home. Everyone seemed to know him because this was one of those pubs – and they were everywhere in those days – where local servants met during their time off. Only male servants that is. In the 1920s the only women who went in pubs on their own – I mean unaccompanied by men – were prostitutes or at least that's what people said. Men seemed to resent the presence of women, which seemed odd to me even then. The other thing about pubs in those days was that many of them would attract people from one walk of life only – so a servants' pub would hardly ever have a customer who was not a servant, a market porters' pub would be filled only with porters and so on. I remember once going in a coal heavers' pub and when I looked through the door all faces turned to me and it was like the old black and white minstrel show – not a face was there but was black as night but with huge white eyes!

Anyway, as we entered the Footman's Rest George shouted greetings across at various people who were standing at the bar or sitting at the few tables round about.

He ordered two large whiskies at the bar while I shifted about uneasily next to him. When the drinks arrived he sloshed some water into both, said cheers and downed a great gulp of his. I reached for my glass just as the barman said – looking carefully and directly at me – 'That will be ninepence,' or whatever it was.

This was clearly a regular ruse of George's because the barman was in on it. I didn't mind at all because I was the new boy and at least everyone here was friendly. I handed over the money.

But the whisky brought me to my senses. As soon as I finished it and thought it was time to be off I resolved to avoid going to the pub, any pub, in future with George. He had the look of a serious drinker. I'd grown up in a house where the perils of drink was a constant theme and I never felt completely comfortable in any pub, not even with Billy and the odd pint of weak beer.

But before I could go George had found a table and he continued chatting to me as if he'd known me forever. He even whipped out his snuff tin and offered me a pinch, perhaps to make up for getting me to pay for the drinks.

After about half an hour I had plucked up the courage to tell him I had to leave. I stood up and said, 'I've got to get back. Sorry.'

Without another word George leapt up and said, 'Of course.'

He waved to a few people and we left. He accompanied me all the way to the station and when he left me he said he was looking forward to working with me as I would be under him. And that was that. I went back home and handed my notice to Mr Carter. He wasn't the least bit perturbed because male servants tended to leave to better themselves – or at least they left more often than the women servants, many of whom stayed for life in the same house.

James was sad to see me go and said so. He also said he'd be seeing me soon up in town but of course he never did.

My mother said she was proud of me. I packed my own box, James drove me to the station and that was it: I had said goodbye to my childhood home.

Chapter 16

My two main reasons for going to London were money, as I've said, and girls. As I was moving up from junior footman to second footman my wages went up a bit and there was some extra money because the job was in London.

But even the money paled into insignificance next to the lure of the girls James had talked about. I thought the streets would be littered with beautiful young women all looking for a fine young footman for a husband. You see I was very conventional – I might have been desperate for a girl but I wanted to do the right thing. I didn't know anyone then who thought they could get a girlfriend without intending to marry her. It just wasn't done where I came from. What an innocent I was! Back home if you'd gone out with a girl and tried to sleep with her before you got married, her dad would be around in five minutes to skin you alive. Then he'd tell your dad what you were up to and he'd join in and skin you a bit more. But I was in my late twenties and thought I'm going to go mad if I don't find someone.

Inevitably of course London was a bit of a disappointment. The streets weren't paved with girls or, if they were, I never really had time to get out and see many of them. And at first I was very lonely because I'd gone from a place where I knew almost everyone and everyone knew me to a place where I was completely unknown. I was just another domestic servant among thousands of others.

And London taught me another lesson. Back home I'd never had the sense that servants were looked down on by the wider world because there was no wider world. On the estate, apart from the family, we were *all* servants of one kind or another. The butler might have looked down on the hall boy and the cook might have looked down on the scullery maid, but people in other trades and jobs round about didn't give you the feeling of being inferior. In London it was very different and even factory girls tended to see servants as a waste of time. And office workers and clerks looked at you as if they'd trodden in something.

Mind you, the only time I came across a group of factory girls they scared the life out of me. I'd walked up to Camden on my afternoon off and was daydreaming as I passed a group of girls outside the famous cigarette factory at Mornington Crescent. I'd obviously let my gaze linger a bit too long because one or two of them started to shout at me.

'Hello darling,' they bellowed. 'Does your mum know you're out on yer own? Give us a butcher's! Bet you've never 'ad a girl 'ave yer?' and on and on they went like that till I almost ran past them.

Despite girls the likes of which I'd never seen before and the long hours I worked in the house I did eventually fall in love. It was a year or more after I arrived and I had a great deal more to learn in the meantime about the difference between being a footman in the country and a footman in town.

The first thing I had to learn, said George, was that the Dowager was a mad old duck but very kind to the servants who could put up with her. I discovered he was right. Despite the fact that she didn't drink at all she insisted that beer should be served at all meals for the servants, for the girls and the men.

George used to do a great impersonation of the Dowager addressing the butler on the subject of beer.

'Give them beer, Chapman. Water is so debilitating. Do you know, they still draw it from the river? Impenetrably stupid. Filled with noxious Germanic chemicals. The very idea makes one's personality shudder. Beer, Chapman, beer is the thing. Well boiled it is a moral balsam, excellent for hysterical girls.'

I used to become hysterical myself with laughing when he did this sort of thing. He was an immensely talented mimic and you have to imagine it delivered by a great tall thin gangling thing. But I was upset one day when I heard him mimicking *my* country accent, which I thought I'd lost. And the effect was made all the funnier because he apparently also mimicked a slight tendency I had to sway back and forth while I spoke. But even when he was mocking you it was hard not to like him. Despite his natural stoop he was always ramrod straight when he stood at the back of the dining room or was in the presence of any member of the family. Like many of us he was two different people: the servant, who was quiet and dignified and deferential, and the private individual who liked a drink and gave free rein to his eccentricities.

George seemed to have worked all over the place. He told me once about a big house in the country where he had worked for some years.

'It was bloody mad, bloody mad all the time,' he said, 'but we had some laughs. The kitchen was so far from the bloody dining room that we had to run about a quarter of a mile to get the food there before it was cold. Eventually they fitted an iron safe outside the dining room. It was heated with coal and here the plates were kept nice and hot, but we'd got so used to running from the kitchen that we kept at it when there was no longer any need. We'd race each other praying the old butler wouldn't come out and catch us. But they hated the servants there – really hated them. They'd spent thousands of pounds building a tunnel under the front gardens of the house so that the servants could go in and out without ever being seen by the family looking out of the drawing-room window or other rooms at the front of the house. And the tunnel came up and out on a different part of the road from the main drive to the house.'

George was also famously foul-mouthed. He was always saying, 'The trouble with servant girls is they love fucking.' Or he'd say: 'I got her up against the wall and she was so gone she almost fainted.'

At first I thought it was all talk, but it wasn't. George was so confident and direct and unselfconscious that I think the girls, or at least some of them, were mesmerised by him.

Chapter 17

A week after I arrived to start work I was told by George that the Dowager wished to see me. 'You'll enjoy this,' he said with a big ridiculous grin.

I trotted up the stairs and knocked on the drawing-room door and a surprisingly girlish voice immediately said, 'Come in.'

I opened the door, made a little bow, and said, 'You asked for me, madam?'

She was much older than I had imagined from her voice and very thin. She wore a dress that looked long out of date and with a very low neckline which was odd to say the least in someone so elderly – I guessed she was in her seventies. She had grey hair piled elaborately on her head and a very pale complexion with a large number of moles dotted here and there so that she looked rather like a currant bun.

She was seated in a large wicker armchair surrounded by cushions and smoking a cigarette, which was still considered rather racy in those days. I also noticed that she had a second cigarette burning on the edge of an ashtray and she had an open fan in her left hand. Behind her in a rack were at least fifteen umbrellas and parasols. She looked me up and down.

'I do hope you will be happy here,' she said. 'We have strict rules but they are fair rules. You were in Hertfordshire before I believe. A rather backward place in many respects. I am sorry for you. Here we keep up, we are up to date so far as is compatible with position. But I must warn you. I will have no talk, no talk at all. Chatter is damaging to morale and to health. Do not chatter to the girls. Do not chatter to me. Do not chatter in the garden. Do not chatter when you are alone or in company. Thank you for coming to see me.' With that she turned in her seat. I bowed and began my retreat.

As I reached the door she said, 'I hope you enjoy beer? We drink only beer here. I drink it myself.'

'I do indeed enjoy beer,' I said

'I am glad to hear it,' she said, 'or we would have been at loggers.'

Back at home in the country the senior male staff – the first footman and butler – had slept in their own rooms. Here in London things were rather different. The first and junior footmen and I slept in a musty old room along with the hall boy. We were in an old storage room that ran from the house out under the street. The room had a row of small bull's-eye windows set into the ceiling to allow a little light in from the public footpath overhead. We slept on folding beds and it was always damp. There was no heating and only one oil lamp on a table near the door. We kept our clothes in a long cupboard that ran from floor to ceiling and wall to wall on the side of the room opposite the bull's-eye glass. Inside the cupboard there were, as well as our everyday suits, ceremonial suits and wigs and in a corner were several sets of leather coachman's capes and huge coachman's boots that might have been a century old and were clearly never used now.

It was a gloomy, depressing room and made worse because George used to shout out in his sleep every night and because the hall boy could sometimes be heard crying in the early hours. I asked him several times if he was all right and he insisted he was fine. He can't have been more than twelve and I think he missed his parents. We all slept in our clothes or at least some of them. We'd take off our uniform suits and put our own trousers and shirts back on. It was cold in winter and getting up at 6 a.m. on an icy day in December was unbelievable agony. I would often walk around the room shivering uncontrollably until I started to keep my uniform in bed with me. I risked someone noticing that it was a bit creased but having it in bed with me kept it warm and reduced the shock of dressing in January.

We three footmen each had a basin of water to shave in brought to us by the hall boy who had to get up first, poor devil.

Wherever you worked male servants always slept downstairs or in the basement to keep them as far as possible from the female servants, who slept in the attic rooms. Of course if a male servant and one of the girls were determined to meet nothing would stop them. And I quickly realised that it wasn't always true that a girl wouldn't have sex with a man before marriage. In those more repressed days girls as well as men would occasionally break out whatever the risks, and they did it in ways that never happened once women were officially liberated in the 1960s. It was a question of sheer physical appetite eventually getting the better of the terror of pregnancy.

I remember meeting one of the girls in a corridor of the house basement where she shouldn't really have been. She had a strange intent look on her face and hardly noticed me as she passed. Ten minutes later I was coming back along the same passage and heard a noise coming from a storeroom just off the corridor. I stopped, unsure of what it was – I was such an innocent! I could hear gasping and low, intense, repeated moans and I stood transfixed thinking, 'What on earth is that?'

Though I had no experience at all of sex the truth suddenly dawned on me and I knew what this was. The moans gathered pace and became louder and I hurried away thinking I'd get caught if I hung about any longer. I discovered that it was George with Grace, the girl I'd passed a little earlier in the corridor. For a long time I couldn't really believe it because Grace was about four feet ten tall and George, as I've said, was about six feet ten. The third footman used to say to me, 'That George is as randy as a goose, but how the fuck he does it with Grace I just don't know. Should we ask him do you think? Does she stand on a stepladder?'

Chapter 18

It's hard to describe a typical day in that house but it was much livelier and less predictable than a day back at the estate would have been and a lot of this had to do with the Dowager herself.

After the maids had laid the fires in the sitting room and drawing room in winter we would take up position in the dining room, having carried up and set the breakfast things. In many families the dishes would be on a sideboard and the family would help themselves, but the Dowager liked to have absolutely everything done for her. So while the first footman was downstairs with the butler she would insist that I stood to attention, ready in case she needed anything. She always asked me rather than the junior footman who just stood silently throughout breakfast and was never asked for anything. He was a good-looking boy and much more of an ornament than I was.

After breakfast had been cleared we would retreat downstairs and relax for a while but as often as not the Dowager would have made it known through the butler or the first footman that she wanted to walk in the park.

We had to endure this at least twice a week and it was usually my role to accompany her. George was too important for the job. He had to spend the morning cleaning the silver. And the junior footman Charles was perhaps too young and inexperienced.

Tuesdays and Thursdays were the Dowager's usual walking days and I was instructed to stand at the side of the front hall near the front door, ready for her arrival there at ten o'clock. If it had been fifty years earlier, or perhaps even thirty, I would have had to powder my hair and wear gold britches and white silk stockings but the Dowager was fairly keen on modern ideas including the idea that her footmen should wear a simple dark suit. I rather liked the suit, too, though it was a heavy woollen affair and the unlined trousers scratched and itched horribly. She paid for the suit and I received a new one every two years, made especially for me.

George had explained the routine. As soon as the Dowager arrived in the hall I was to open the front door, step outside and then wait slightly to the left. The Dowager would then come out and hand me her spaniel's lead. I would then turn and close the front door. 'She's a stickler for routine,' said George. 'Stand on the wrong side of the door and she'll kick you in the shins!'

As she descended the steps on to the footpath I was to stay just behind and still to the left, carrying her umbrella or on warm days her parasol. I was not to speak to her unless spoken to first.

What amazed me the first time I went on this walk was that there were always several other women in the park – sometimes half a dozen – being trailed by dour-looking footmen in similar black outfits.

The Dowager would occasionally stop and talk to one of these women for a few moments before moving on. She neither spoke to me nor looked in my direction until she had reached a certain point in the walk, which varied from time to time. Then she would announce, 'I think that will do for today,' and she would turn for home. At this point I was supposed to pick the dog up, which I duly did. We trailed back to the house where she waited at the steps until I had run up and rung the bell. The butler let us in and took the dog. The dog was placed on the ground, the Dowager came through the door, I closed the door and the butler returned the lead and the attached dog to the Dowager. If it could have been done without impropriety – that was a word they all loved back then – I swear she'd have had me carry her up the stairs.

The first time we went through all this I realised how extraordinarily tiny and thin she was. Like a sort of underfed sparrow and undoubtedly below five feet tall. In the daylight she looked terribly old – far older than when I'd seen her the first time in the drawing room and God knows she'd looked old enough then. None of the staff seemed to know who she was related to or if she'd ever been married at all. There was some talk of an Irish estate but none of us had ever been sent there and the Dowager herself went only to her country house.

One of the funniest trips to the park happened that first summer when I was asked to carry an umbrella *and* a parasol as the weather was changeable. The Dowager's dog normally did its business in the flower beds and no one in those days cleaned up after their dogs. The dog was called Dash after one of Queen Victoria's dogs and it was very overweight which is why it always had to be carried back. I was about to pick up Dash after it had been to the loo when another dog appeared at high speed from nowhere and attacked Dash. I was so surprised that I stood stupidly holding the lead while Dash ran in small circles in terror while a much larger nondescript sort of hound snapped and snarled at it. In an instant after that I felt the parasol snatched from under my arm. The Dowager had been transformed into a young avenger. She began beating the bigger dog with all her might while shouting, 'You bastard! I will teach you to attack my dog. How dare you!' The old lady seemed remarkably athletic for someone who had previously never moved at more than a snail's pace. And it worked. The hound was as astonished as me. It backed off, yelping, as she continued to thwack it about the ears. A moment later the dog's owner, a rough-looking man with an enormous military moustache, trotted up to us and shouted, 'Come off it, Gyp.'

The Dowager stepped in front of the man, who was

twice her size, and said: 'Your dog is an animal, sir, and so are you!'

The man laughed and began to walk off at which the old lady strode right up to him and began to hit *him* around the head and shoulders with her parasol. He was so amazed that he simply ran off with his dog trotting behind.

Now I thought I would be in a lot of trouble after that as I had done nothing to save the dog or chastise its owner, but the Dowager simply returned the parasol to me, smiled to herself and set off for home with me trailing miserably behind.

At lunch that day I was convinced I would be asked to remain below stairs rather than stand in the dining room and I dreaded the butler telling me I had been summoned upstairs, but nothing happened. The day went on as before. I carried the lunch up and the dirty plates back down and then had a little time off before preparations for dinner began.

Neither the servants nor the Dowager ever referred to the incident.

Two days later I had ceased to worry, but the business with the dog in the park was typical of her eccentricities. When I mentioned it to George, in a version of the story that made me look a little more useful, he wasn't in the least surprised. He told me that she was famous for assaulting cab drivers, the postman and anyone who irritated her. But she would always immediately forget all about it. He said that there had been a terrific fuss when he had answered a knock at the door one morning about a year before I arrived.

'I opened the door just a little, which is what the old lady always insisted on. She thinks if the door is opened wide each time it will let Germans in – she means germs but she always refers to them as Germans. Anyway I opened the door and there was a policeman standing there who asked to see the Dowager. He explained that there had been a complaint from a tradesman who said he had been hit by a woman carrying an umbrella. He had identified the woman as the Dowager.

'I went to the drawing room and told her that there was a policeman at the front door and that he wanted to see her. She told me to tell him to go to the tradesman's entrance. So I traipsed back to the front door and passed on the message. The bobby was red in the face by now but the power of the upper classes got the better of him and he marched down the steps and round the back. I went back to the Dowager and asked her what I should do next.

'"Tell him to go away," she said. So that's what I did. And he went off saying that if the person who had made the complaint insisted on bringing an action then the Dowager would be summoned to the magistrate's court. I went back to her ladyship and began to explain what he had said. She raised her hand to silence me, said "Don't be absurd," and dismissed me. She might be a mad old duck but she couldn't care less about the Old Bill and you have to admire her for that!'

And nothing did ever come of the complaint. As George was always pointing out, you'd have to murder someone in front of the prime minister to get arrested if you were upper class and I was to see this sort of contempt for the law several times in my career – once, spectacularly, in a job I took after leaving the house in Regent's Park.

Chapter 19

The Dowager rarely had guests to the house and when she did they were always elderly and never more than seven or eight in number I think. When she was dining alone she either sat at the end of the long beautiful walnut table in a room that overlooked the park or more usually she had her dinner taken to her bedroom where, at seven on most evenings, she sat up in bed reading. She played cards with a few elderly female friends one or two evenings a week and that was her life.

We footmen stood silently each evening at the edge of the dimly lit room tending the fires occasionally, bringing tea or drinks and then returning to our places. Imagine the madness of it – three evenings a week the head footman and I would stand at the back of the dining room or the drawing room for two or three hours without moving except to hand something to the Dowager or put another log on the fire. It was so dull and the whole point of her life doing nothing was presumably to make the Dowager think always that she was a cut above the rest. She could have cut her bills and had one footman – it would have been more than enough, but it would never have occurred to her. We were like Russian serfs: the more of us you had the higher your status. George told me about houses where there were four footmen kept hanging about for hours just in case someone with a title – as George put it – needed to have their noses scratched once or twice in an evening.

We longed more than anything to escape because we were not allowed out of the house except on business and on our afternoons off. I had Tuesday afternoons free and every other Sunday which was good by the standards of the time. Older staff told me that when they had started they often had no time off for weeks and months. Time off was given only at the discretion of the butler and housekeeper, who wanted to appear diligent in the eyes of their employers, so they hardly gave any time off at all in case they were accused of being over-generous.

After about a year in the Regent's Park house I had made some friends by visiting the local pub where I was told the younger footmen gathered. This was not the pub where I had been taken by George on my first day in London. I avoided going anywhere with George as he always made me pay and senior footmen tended to mix only with footmen on the same level – unless they were trying to get them to pay for the drinks. My favourite pub, and I became very fond of it, was the haunt of junior footmen and second footmen only.

I began to look forward to my evenings at the King's, which was just off Marylebone Road. Being a footman made you part of a club and you felt almost immediately close to other footmen with whom you could swap stories. After only ever hearing stories about people in a limited country circle, I loved the outrageous gossip I heard in that pub. And I went there for the five years and more I stayed at that house. I hardly ever missed a Tuesday because after the drab routine of domestic service the King's meant freedom and fun – even for someone like me who spent the whole evening with half a pint of mild. I occasionally drank more than I should but temporary freedom and drink are a heady combination. Most of the footmen I met were heavy drinkers because I think they had to be so buttoned-up and in control when they were at work.

I wish I could remember all the wonderful stories I heard in the King's because they brightened up my life no end and made me feel I had made a great decision in coming to London. It was also here that I met Dermot O'Halloran, always known as Derry, who became my friend for life. And it was through Derry that some time later I met Alice.

Chapter 20

The great thing about Derry was that he was always full of plans and schemes. Like me he was from the country, and like me he loved his weekly visit to the King's. He was second footman in a house on the other side of the park and we always had a great laugh when we met at the pub. He was tall like all footmen, but dark-skinned, almost Spanish-looking and with astonishingly blue eyes that somehow always looked surprised. They were what we used to call goggle eyes – they sort of bulged a bit. I was at the bar of the King's one night a few months after I'd started work. I'd escaped from George for the umpteenth time by saying I just didn't like his pub.

As I waited to be served I glanced to my left and a man about my own age smiled at me and said, 'If you get served first get me a pint would you and I'll give you the money?'

I thought here we go, another sponger like George, but even as he asked me to buy his drink he pushed fourpence into my hand and smiled.

As it happened I *was* the first to be served and I bought us two drinks and wondered what on earth I should say next. While I was dithering with the change my new friend said, 'Now, I would say you have to be a footman like me – you have that look of supreme intelligence about you.'

I laughed. 'You're right. I am. How on earth did you know?'

'It's something to do with the way you look. As if you want to run around shouting and screaming and throwing your beer all over the place.'

Within two minutes we were chatting away like old friends and two hours later a little the worse for wear we swaggered out into the night to make sure we were back at our houses before the ten o'clock curfew. We all knew the rules and we had to be up mighty early.

'Don't let them see you've had a few!' shouted Derry when he left me at the edge of the park. 'See you next week.'

I said that Derry was always full of plans and schemes and I meant it. He had a bicycle which was a rare thing then. Very expensive. He'd saved for a year to buy it and on his days off he cycled miles out of London to all sorts of interesting places. The great days of the bicycle had been from about 1895 to just before the Great War. After the war the rich had lost interest in bicycles because cars were the new exciting thing, but for the less well off – and you needed to be fabulously wealthy to have the least chance of buying a car – bicycles meant freedom and excitement.

After listening to Derry's thrilling tales of hurtling down the hills of Surrey and Middlesex I decided I would save to buy a bicycle. I just had to have one. This didn't actually take all that long because I had been saving anyway.

My weekly expenditure was not much at all because I was given a new suit when I started the job and I had all my food included – and of course accommodation. But a bike was still expensive, especially if you consider that a motorbike at this time could cost more than a small terraced house! I remember gazing at a motorbike in a showroom that cost £150, three times my annual wages. I reckon a new three-speed Sturmey Archer bicycle was around £10 then and that was a pretty basic model.

I had a stroke of luck when I set my heart on a bike because Derry told me a few weeks after we started to discuss it that he knew someone who was selling an older bike for £5. Of course I jumped at the chance and met Derry and his friend a few weeks later on my Sunday off and the deal was done.

Now began one of the happiest periods of my life. It was as much fun as my evenings in the pub, but much more exhilarating. When you've hardly been on a train, never in a car and never on a motorbike, you can't imagine the excitement of learning to ride your own bike. I wasn't the least embarrassed at being nearly thirty and only just learning because bicycles weren't seen at all as things for children then. You often saw older people learning to ride in the park.

Later on when far more people could afford a car there was a view that anyone on a bike wasn't on it because they wanted the exercise or enjoyed cycling. No, by the 1950s and 1960s if you were on a bike everyone thought it was because you couldn't afford a car. But in the 1930s the bike was still a marvel, a thing that ordinary people wanted desperately to own because it was within reach and gave unimagined freedom.

Derry helped me learn by running behind me and holding the saddle, and at first I felt such an unwieldy lump on that contraption. After my first lesson in what they called the inner ring – really just a quiet circular road through Regent's Park – I was convinced I would never get the hang of it. It was just too difficult. How could you not topple over on this great heavy thing that rested on two slippery wheels that were just an inch across?

But Derry was encouraging – as well as extremely abusive about my lack of ability.

As I cycled along he would shout, 'Go faster you idiot. Don't lean. Not that way. Jesus in a bucket! Toes on the pedals not your bloody heels.'

Once he shouted, 'It's like trying to teach a fucking hippo!' and I laughed so much I fell off immediately and lay on the grass unable to speak for ten minutes. But he was laughing too. Secretly I enjoyed having this thing to try to master. I had a great motivation to learn too because Derry and I had discussed all the places we would go and all the things we'd do.

'But we can't do a single one of them till you stop falling on your arse,' he would say.

On the third Sunday after I'd begun my lessons we were going along and as usual I was wobbling all over the place and could hear poor Derry panting along beside and a little behind me. I pushed on a bit and something seemed to change. I was able to lean and correct a near overbalance. I thought I could feel something different so I applied the brake, came to a halt and excitedly told Derry.

'You bloody clot,' he said.

'What do you mean?' I replied, offended. 'I thought you'd be pleased I at least kept going a bit.'

'But did you not notice anything else that time?' he asked with a grin.

'What? Tell me what or I'll push you in the lake.'

'For the last couple of minutes that time you were completely on your own. I wasn't holding the saddle at all.'

I was so delighted I couldn't say a word.

'You can stop that bloody grinning because now we have to sort out where we're going,' said Derry.

Chapter 21

It seemed very difficult to get through a week of dull standing and serving, standing and serving, watching endless card games and even duller dinners and breakfasts. I thought the next Sunday would never come around. In the meantime I tried to concentrate on the odd things that happened now and then to liven life up a bit even in the worst week. I can remember in the days leading up to our first bicycle adventure the Dowager seemed to change gear. She had broken out of her ancient routine.

I remember hearing the cook say: 'She's been down here twice today. What the hell's she doing? I can't cook under these bloody conditions.' She was walking up and down in a foul mood, throwing her arms about and slamming down pots and pans.

I'd never seen anything like this before. Then the butler appeared and Cook quietened down a bit, such was the power of the head of the servants. He was very good. He led her out of the kitchen to his room and she didn't reappear for half an hour, by which time she was perfectly calm and quietly got on with her cooking. I later heard that the butler had promised to discuss a pay rise for her, something that would never be done for more lowly staff. Cooks were starting to be hard to get and I know that the butler was perfectly capable of telling the Dowager off if she caused trouble below stairs, especially with the cook, because he knew her value.

A week later Cook was wandering round beaming and we all knew she'd had her pay!

The great Sunday arrived and it was time for my first real adventure with Derry. I'd got the hang of the bicycle completely on my last Wednesday afternoon off. In fact I'd kept at it so long I had blisters on my bum. But now it was time to go further afield. 'You've got to be ambitious on a bike,' as Derry put it.

I was allowed to keep my bicycle in an outbuilding that had been a stable so I collected it and pushed it carefully towards the end of the street where the traffic roared along the Marylebone Road. I say carefully because that bicycle was my only really valuable possession and I treated it like it was as delicate as a piece of china!

Then, while I was walking along pushing my sparkling machine (I'd cleaned and recleaned it every chance I got), and a short way before I reached the main road, a girl stepped into my path from one of the big houses. She just appeared out of a doorway and turned to face me for a moment. She looked me very directly in the eyes, smiled an enormous blue-eyed smile and walked past.

I'd long ago given up the idea that London was filled with girls just waiting for me and all my attention recently had of course been on the bicycle but fate had decided to take a hand.

In the long years that have passed since that day I've often wondered what might have happened if I'd left the house ten minutes later or ten minutes earlier. I would never have seen Alice, which used to make me almost panic when I thought of it. I used to try to convince myself that it would not have been a disaster, that I might have seen her on another day. I had to reassure myself by saying that because otherwise what happened to the rest of my life might have happened for someone else or for no one.

As she went on her way I turned and watched her go. And in the way of these things I noticed absolutely every detail about her and I have always remembered every detail. Much of what happens in everyone's lives slips by and is quickly forgotten but everyone has a few moments, perhaps often seemingly trivial moments, when the details seem almost ridiculously vivid and they never fade. This for me was one of those moments.

She was about five feet three inches tall and with narrow delicate shoulders and hips. You hardly ever saw a fat person in those far-off days – or if you did, it was odds on it was a cook or chef. But there was something wonderful about Alice's shape and size, the way she held her head, the way she turned. And she walked in a very beautiful, delicate way that I find almost impossible to describe. It was the way I imagine trained dancers might walk, but poor Alice never had a dancing lesson in her life. Then again, she didn't need one.

That first time I saw her face it was only for an instant but I never forgot the moment and fifty years later it still came back to my mind regularly and each time it was as if I was standing by the side of the road again with that heavy old bike leaning on me.

She had an oval face and very fair, almost child-like skin with light freckles across the bridge of her nose and under her eyes. Her eyes, which seemed slightly too big for her face, were pale blue. She had very fine, but not at all thin fair hair, not pale or almost white, but a sort of dark corn colour, very smooth and straight and beautifully twisted into a loose bun behind her head.

I was completely smitten and in a way that was almost painful. I was instantly terrified I would not see her again. Many times since I have tried to work out why she appealed to me so overwhelmingly and I can't do it because it was all her features and her smile taken together. Even a photograph would not do her justice because it was the fact of her moving and being alive that brought all the separate things I have tried to describe into one unique whole.

It's so strange, isn't it, that when you fall in love you often remember a tiny, silly detail. I remembered lots of details on that first occasion: her freckles, her eyes, her shoulders and the way she had tied that bun at the back of her head. Unlike most servant girls – and I knew straight away she was a servant – she hadn't made her hair fiercely tidy or scraped back like a dancer's.

She had tied it back with a casual air so it was loose and a few strands blew about as she walked. I remember thinking, 'How does she get away with that?' It was almost as if she was not working for someone else at all. It was as if she was on her day off which she clearly wasn't because she was wearing a maid's uniform. But the hair was part of her relaxed charm and I was convinced – and later found it to be true – that she charmed everyone, even her employers, who dreaded the thought of losing her.

The truth is that she was that rare thing – an ordinary girl who had a sort of natural aristocratic air to her that wasn't to do with arrogance or money, but to do with quiet confidence and intelligence.

Now girls often thought that boys – even other servant boys – would never want to go out with them because there was some shame attached to being a servant girl. Alice wasn't embarrassed about anything, least of all being a servant. And as a result of her looks and her happy confidence in herself, it was impossible, for me at least, to imagine her not being pursued by every man in London.

* * *

But on that first morning, having stared into the distance long after she had disappeared along the road, I suddenly remembered what I was supposed to be doing. I tried to throw all thoughts of Alice off and pushed my bike the last few dozen yards to the spot where I was to meet Derry.

The sun came out, the traffic roared and Derry appeared smiling broadly, but my mind was elsewhere. For a while Derry didn't notice. He showed me proudly a small canvas bag that had sandwiches for our lunch and explained that we were going to cycle to Hertfordshire.

It was only that word recalling my home county that brought me to my senses.

We cycled off westwards through the cars and cabs, the buses and lorries. At this time it was a mixture of horse-drawn vehicles (though fewer now) and the new motor vehicles. But the variety of cars and lorries then was amazing. I remember seeing a van whose sides were made of mahogany and brass! That sort of thing was really common back then because the coach builders who made cars, buses and lorries were the same coach builders who had made the transition from the old horse-drawn vehicles. Lots of the old techniques were carried over, which is why you regularly saw wooden lorries. They were beautiful things and in some cases the chassis and the coachwork were separate, so back at the depot they'd lift off the van and put a different top on the chassis for different work.

So off we went, weaving (in my case wobbling) through miles of traffic out through Paddington and then up the Edgware Road. Half a mile away from central London and the traffic had almost dried up. You'd see miles of suburban houses and streets with just one or two cars in them. Cars were just too expensive for most people and the few very rich people who did have cars tended to live in central London, not in those little terraced houses that spread for mile after mile in the suburbs. Suburban streets would empty in the morning as everyone caught the seven-thirty train or the underground and then the streets would sleep the day away with hardly a sound beyond the milk van and the coal merchant – usually still using horses.

By the time we reached Willesden we were in deep countryside and the narrow lanes seemed to climb forever, to remote villages and tiny medieval churches. I'd never been much interested in old buildings but Derry was a bit of an expert and he made me see how lovely these things were even as they were being demolished.

We saw two old village ponds being filled in by workmen on that first outing and several village streets we passed through were having major work done, whole rows of ancient buildings were coming down, usually to widen the roads. There was a mania for building at the time. We all thought it was a good thing, then – well, everyone except Derry who thought it was terrible, which was eccentric at the time. If you came from the countryside as I did the last thing you wanted was a few old houses round a pond and no life – you wanted cars and cinemas, modern buildings and houses and shops. It was only when most of the quiet villages of London's western suburbs were gone that we started to wish we hadn't given them over to the car! I don't think it took us more than an hour to reach real countryside.

I remember at one stage we cycled along a track that wound for miles across the hills of north London and we hardly saw a soul. Then we passed under a railway viaduct and the roar of a train overhead, the smoke and rattle surprised us so much we stopped to listen. It was a reminder that London was still close by, though it seemed so far. Then on we went for at least another half mile with the trees meeting overhead and not a passerby to be seen. Decades later after I retired and when poor Derry was long dead I tried to follow our old route but it was impossible. There were trunk roads everywhere, huge roundabouts and industrial buildings and estates. I recognised nothing. It was sad.

We stopped eventually at a small pub on a road that was eventually, I think, to become the A1. A few people sat at tables on the beaten earth at the front of the pub. The building itself was brick and timber, a long low thing that leaned forward at a precarious angle. Inside, the stone-flagged floor was at least eighteen inches lower than the road outside. It was very dark with a massively bowed ceiling just a few feet overhead and there were at least four tiny bars each filled with dark furniture that looked as if it had been there for a century and more. I remember looking out of the window across the small fields to a wood while Derry went to the bar for two glasses of mild, a weak watery beer that was refreshing but didn't make you in the least bit drunk. It was also very cheap!

After we left the pub we carried on roughly heading away from London and always, it seemed, climbing higher and higher until there came a point where we looked back and there was London spread out before us but tiny now and miles away.

I knew so little about the world that I thought once we reached Hertfordshire I would see the old estate but of course Hertfordshire is a big county and we were nowhere near it.

I cycled behind Derry who was confident and of course knew the way, which I did not. He'd cycled this way many times he told me, but he seemed to know all the routes out of London. I told him that he should write a book, but despite his great interest in the world and his great intelligence he actually struggled to write the simplest note.

As we rode along he would shout back at me continually about the things we were passing. He seemed to know so much about everything, but when we stopped for lunch – the wonderful sandwiches he'd brought – he said:

'You don't seem yourself.'

'Oh I'm in the pink,' I said, but inside I knew that for much of the time we'd been bowling along my mind had been drawn back again and again to the fair-haired girl I'd seen that morning.

'You are not fine at all,' said Derry. 'You only replied about half the times I spoke to you even when we were cycling side by side.'

'Are you sure?' I said.

'Of course I'm sure!'

'Oh well, I'm just a bit excited by all this bicycle riding.'

'Crikey. It's a bloomin' girl isn't it?'

I must have blushed because he said, 'I don't know why you'd make a fuss. We all get it now and then when we see someone. Who is she?'

'I don't know,' I said. 'I only saw her for the first time this morning as I walked down to meet you.'

I told him what she looked like and where she'd suddenly appeared.

'Oh that's Alice,' he said. 'Everyone fancies her!'

I stood open-mouthed and I must admit slightly aggrieved that he should say such a thing about her. Isn't that terrible? I already thought I had a say in what people thought about her.

He explained that he himself had spoken to Alice a couple of times when she was meeting one of the maids who worked in his house. That shows what a closed little world the servant world was. The footmen and butlers had their pubs and bars and the maids walked out together in the parks or met for tea.

'Does she have someone?' I asked.

'I don't think so, but I've no idea really. She works

round the park somewhere. I often see her when I'm out and about. I'm sure Alice's friend – the maid in my house – will help if you really want to meet her.'

And that was that. We turned for home with my head full of Alice and soon the woods and lanes were behind us and we were home, if home is what you can call it.

Chapter 22

Living in someone else's house takes a lot of getting used to. You never really relax except perhaps when you are asleep and maybe not even then for footmen were occasionally woken in the middle of the night.

Apart from its being someone else's house, there was nothing at all wrong with the house in Regent's Park and though the Dowager was, as George had said, a mad old duck, I was being paid well and there wasn't a lot to do except stand still in the dining room, throw logs on the fire and carry dishes up- and downstairs, but I was still ambitious and longed for promotion and enough money to think that one day I might be able to marry. And now of course I had someone I wanted to marry.

I was determined to find a way to meet Alice. Once I'd done that I thought that if I could get a better position near at hand and with more money she would be impressed and I might find a way to ask her for a date. In the meantime I was in an agony that she might meet someone else or might already be going out with somebody else.

I'm no expert but I'd guess that everyone through-out history who has been in love or obsessed with someone had the same fears as I did then. They were horribly distracting and they affected my work. Mr Chapman told me off a few times for not concentrating and once I committed a cardinal sin: I dropped a china bowl. I was convinced I'd have my wages docked and get a severe telling-off, but Mr Chapman told me that the Dowager wouldn't even notice and not to worry about it, which was decent of him and unusual. Butlers were usually sticklers for that sort of thing.

Chapter 23

My mind was taken temporarily off Alice when I was told I had to accompany the Dowager to her country house. I knew nothing about this house but with several other servants we were sent on ahead one autumn to prepare for her arrival. We went by train, third class of course. The butler supervised the dozens of heavy leather suitcases, trunks and boxes that were carried to the station, but he wasn't to come up till later. The Dowager's favourite silver even had to be carried up along with all sorts of things she couldn't do without. There were dressing cases and several trunks of clothes. Each dress and shirt and skirt was lined with tissue paper inside and out before being carefully laid in the trunks by the Dowager's lady's maid, Grace, who was older even than the Dowager herself and had been with her, so legend had it, for more than fifty years. She had the great privilege of travelling second class.

It turned out to be a small, soggy-looking eighteenth-century house just outside Oxford. I say small but in fact it had about ten bedrooms and numerous drawing rooms, studies, smoking rooms and an abandoned nursery in the attic.

While the maids cleaned the rooms and aired the beds I helped with the fires and drew back the old wooden blinds to let the sunlight in. I wandered up the staircase, which was lit by a glass dome in the ceiling. I was really just nosing around. I could, in the absence of the butler to tell me off. I went into several tiny rooms up in the attic which awaited the female servants. Miserable, cold little rooms they were and each painted a dreary green – I thought it was as if the rooms were painted deliberately to stop anyone feeling too cheerful. But perhaps it was just that dark green paint was cheap.

Anyway, I pushed open a door beyond the servants' rooms and there thick with dust lay hundreds of toys scattered across the floor and on three small beds. The smell of damp and mildew was strong and I'm sure there were mice everywhere – you can always smell them. But there was a dead feel to that room despite the toys lying everywhere and clothes spilling out of chests and cupboards. Even the fireplace held the charred remains of a fire that had not been cleaned for years. I noticed dolls, including some with beautiful but eerie china faces, and there were skittles, a dolls' house, a huge box of wooden dolls and of course a rocking horse. It was like a scene from an old story. When I mentioned all this later to the head housemaid she just said, 'Oh, we're not allowed to clean in there. Don't know why and don't care. Less work for us so it suits me.' And that was that. I never found out why it had been left like that, but most old houses had rooms, even whole wings, that were abandoned even before the wealthy began to run out of money.

It was said back in my old home in Hertfordshire that the odd-job man once found a tramp sleeping in an abandoned corner of the house who claimed he'd been sleeping there on and off for six months. The maids never cleaned there, the doors were locked and the tramp had been climbing in through a broken window. My brother told me he'd even been lighting a fire!

At that house in Oxfordshire I made up my bed downstairs in a room near the boot room while we waited the few days till the Dowager was due to arrive. The gardener who lived in an unbelievably small house at the end of the short drive told me what to do and where to go. He was a strange fellow, partly I think because he was alone at the property for most of the year. It was his job to look around the house every day when it was unoccupied to see that no windows were broken, no roof slates had slipped and that everything was watertight. He had little else to do till the Dowager arrived and the fires were lit and flowers were brought in for the tables.

'I always make sure there are flowers,' he said to me. 'That's what she likes and that's what I provide.' And indeed he was really good at this sort of thing.

He had a small glasshouse where he grew all sorts of exotic plants and these, or some of them, were moved into the house when the Dowager arrived.

One day the cook went missing. It was the day after she had arrived. There was a huge ruckus as so much had to be prepared for the arrival of the Dowager. One of the maids told me Cook had flown into a rage on the day they'd left London and hadn't spoken a word to anyone on the train. Then, as I say, a day after arriving at the house she vanished. She came back a couple of days later when we had reached the point of wondering if a new cook would have to be employed. She came into the house, took her coat off and started work without a word. I discovered from one of the maids that she had been into Oxford to a dentist and had all her back teeth taken out. We never found out why but I often wondered if it was a sort of protest against eating and preparing food. She seemed to hate her job.

Cook always seemed to be a mass of pent-up fury. That feeling was common among servants though mostly not in such an extreme form as cooks tended to have it. As a servant you had to be controlled at all times and people did break out occasionally – the strain was too much. I knew a maid in a job I had a few years later who suffered a complete breakdown and was found in the night wandering the corridors wailing and crying without a stitch of clothing on. She had to be committed to an asylum. It wasn't just servants either – most employers were horribly buttoned up too. No one really seemed to let themselves go in those days, certainly not the older people. By the time the Second World War started change was coming and the young began to reject the values of the older generation. They got drunk more often, performed outrageous dances and gave up on all the things their parents had valued. But the effect of all that on us servants was minimal. In the servant world things changed more slowly.

When the Dowager finally turned up she arrived with the butler, Mr Chapman, who told me that she would be shooting in the morning with some friends and that I was to accompany her. The butler said he'd heard that I was from the country so he assumed I would know all about shooting. George was delighted to be passed over because he loved London and hated having to go to 'the wilds' as he called it, especially if he had to do anything out of the house.

'It's just muck, muck and more muck,' he used to say. And, 'When you've fallen in love with one cow, you've fallen in love with them all.'

Next morning I stood at the back of the dining room while the Dowager and a small group of her country friends enjoyed their breakfast. By now I hardly even noticed a word that anyone said other than my friends below stairs. Footmen and butlers learned quickly and without really trying; we learned to drift away in our heads and into whatever thoughts and fancies occupied the time best, but with a tiny alarm still primed to go off instantly if we were addressed directly.

But this time I noticed that they were talking about shooting, which was hard for me to ignore because all those present at breakfast were women. Women did shoot in those days, and more than most people would think, but it was still unusual. More often they accompanied their husbands to watch the action for a bit and then relaxed back in the drawing room before meeting their husbands for lunch. But now it dawned on me that the Dowager, who must have been in her late seventies or early eighties, was planning to shoot right through the morning.

I have to admit I was nervous. I had experience as a loader and of course I'd done lots of shooting myself as a boy, but I had never accompanied a woman before and this particular woman was not in the first flush of youth. Would I be expected to load for her or just hold her cartridge bag? I had no idea.

Shooting is not a dangerous business and it doesn't involve great strength but even a good shot gets knocked about a bit by the recoil from a 12-bore if he or she fires it often enough in a short time. The problem is worse if you are small-framed and using a heavy 12-bore rather than a 16- or 20-bore. As we set off after breakfast I noticed that the Dowager was carrying a 12-bore – she didn't even ask me to carry it. I was half impressed and half appalled.

The shooting brake moved slowly through the woods along a track and then stopped at the first drive. I walked behind the Dowager who amazed me by giving me the gun for a moment, lighting a cigarette and then walking along with it stuck in her mouth, actually hanging from her lower lip. This wasn't just a bit racy. It was revolutionary. It would have been seen as outrageous by the people in the Dowager's set because it was the sort of thing you saw dockers and labourers doing. She was really good at it too because I noticed as I walked discreetly behind her and the others who had now arrived in their cars that she managed to talk without taking the cigarette out of her mouth. It seemed to be glued to her bottom lip.

We reached the meadow at the edge of which those who were shooting took up their positions by their pegs. There were eight shooting and all women, and each with a male servant.

The Dowager seemed to be a changed person from the old lady who did almost nothing in London beyond eat, drink and sleep. She appeared full of energy and most extraordinary of all she was wearing plus fours. This was a shock. I was used to seeing upper-class women dressed in the most traditional fashion – in a way that was essentially still Victorian, with dresses almost to the ground and seemingly layer after layer of material. Yet here was the Dowager alert and in boots and britches and a tight-fitting thick woollen jacket. I rather admired her.

'John, I want you to stand just behind me on the right-hand side,' she said casually after a whistle had been blown somewhere out across the fields to signal the start of the drive. I stepped up until I was a few feet away from her right shoulder. I was behind her and slightly to one side but I had no idea what was going on. She then said, 'When we start would you mind just putting the palm of your hand on my shoulder. Let's see if you can do it.'

I was aghast. We servants were hardly allowed to speak to our employers if we had not been spoken to first and here I was being asked to lay hands on the Dowager.

I reached forward gingerly and put the palm of my hand on the back of her right shoulder.

'No not there,' she said, but not angrily. 'Slightly further back. If you keep a slight pressure it will help when I'm firing.'

I realised what she meant. The push of the heel of the gun into her shoulder – the recoil – as she fired would be lessened if I bolstered her shoulder. I would be absorbing some of the recoil.

So as the first birds came over I increased slightly the pressure of my hand on the back of her shoulder and she began shooting. Now keeping my hand there was difficult because she moved about a bit to fire at the birds at different angles as they came over. Some were directly overhead and some to either side, but as no low birds were allowed to be shot after a while it wasn't that difficult, and when the drive was over she said, 'Well done, John. I think we did rather well.'

And in fact she had done very well. I noticed that she rarely missed and these were fast, high pheasants. The other women had done well too – at least as well as any teams of men I could recall. I'm sure she was less battered as a result of my efforts than she would otherwise have been, but I thought, 'If my father were alive and I told him about this he'd faint!'

This business with the shooting taught me an important lesson. The truth is that you really can't generalise about people. The servants tended to think of their employers as all the same: rigid, obsessed with status and position and above all deeply conventional. In fact the truth was often otherwise. In many respects the people who employed us were deeply unconventional. In later jobs, especially when for a while I became a valet, I discovered something very similar. When you first encountered your employer you simply assumed that he or she was like every other employer and you made the assumption because the rules that governed how we the servants behaved seemed so universal and so narrow. But as you got to know the house, if you worked in the sort of job where you had to have more contact with your employer, you realised that in their own way they were as individual as anyone you might meet at your own level. Of course they also had the time and the money to be extreme individualists if they wanted. The Dowager was a good example.

When the shooting party went back to the house

for lunch the beaters and the loaders and I all trooped off to a barn where we were given beef sandwiches and beer. In the afternoon further shocks awaited me.

The Dowager only ever shot during the mornings so she would shoot on the four morning drives and then lead the beaters in the afternoon. As usual the beaters were all locals. They were unpaid but hoping for a tip at the end of the day or for a bird or two. They didn't look in the least surprised when the Dowager marched up and told them how she wanted the drives to be conducted. I remember she said in a voice like a malevolent sergeant major, 'I don't want anyone to get ahead of the line. You must watch continually left and right to make sure you know where you are. We want a steady stream of good birds.'

I stood to her left this time and on her whistle we began the steady march through the woods, rapping our sticks and hooting to get the birds moving. The Dowager called out now and then in a loud voice, 'Don't get ahead, keep the line, keep the line, don't let them run back,' and so on. For someone elderly and rather small she had a remarkably powerful voice – and it was a voice that was rarely heard in London. Then as we moved steadily forward, one of the beaters who had a spaniel on a leash stumbled and the dog, finding itself free, ran on ahead.

The Dowager immediately roared, 'Get that fucking dog back here this instant. Whose fucking animal is that?' I was more astonished than I have ever been in my life, but even more amazing was the fact that the other beaters hardly seemed to notice. The beater who had slipped whistled up his dog, which was back in a second, and we resumed our march.

I wanted to laugh till I cried but didn't dare. As we walked along the Dowager glanced across at me a few minutes later and I swear she gave me a very slight wink.

Chapter 24

It was winter now and I'd been in my job as second footman for several years. There was London all before me and love was a terrible thing – I was seemingly no nearer a girlfriend than I had ever been. I'm sure this was quite common back then. With so little time off, curfews when you did get a day to yourself and strict rules for men and women servants about no followers, how could it be managed?

Very few girls would sleep with you unless you were married or had agreed to marry. Of course we all heard tales about a footman someone else's footman had heard about who had slept with all the maids, but most of this was just talk. The only person I knew who'd definitely had sex was George. All the others moped and fretted about it as I did.

And besides, I had a girlfriend, or so I liked to think. I clung to this thought despite the fact that she had almost certainly never given *me* another thought after that smile as we passed in the street. I had seen Alice once more in the months that followed my first

bumping into her. Derry told me several time he
would do his best to get us together but neither of us
had any idea how he would do it. I couldn't write a
letter as I didn't even know her surname and she
would probably have run a mile if, out of the blue,
she'd received a letter from someone she didn't know
professing undying love. But day and night for months
on end she filled my thoughts.

Then one afternoon after my half day had been
changed from Tuesday to Wednesday and when I had
almost given up hope I saw her again. I had taken my
usual walk down towards the main road to Marylebone and I saw her again just where I'd seen her the
first time. She was standing on her own, but this time
out of uniform and in a dark blue coat. Her hair was
just as it had been before and it was the thing that
caught my eye.

I must have stopped in some horribly noticeable
way because I could tell she'd seen me. She walked
quickly towards me and said, 'Are you Derry's friend?
He's told me about you. Is this when you usually leave
for your half day?'

'Er . . . yes,' I think I stammered, but I was so taken
aback I could hardly remember a thing later on. I
could tell that I was smiling in a completely false way,
my face like that of a gargoyle, but I couldn't help it.
I just couldn't respond naturally at all.

'That's good,' she said. She smiled and walked
off up the road back the way I had come and towards
the park. Once more I saw that graceful, confident

air she had that was unlike anything I'd ever seen before. The rest of my afternoon off was a blur but that evening I cursed myself for not saying something, anything, vaguely sensible. But what could I do? When I'd had the chance I couldn't say a word. I was so amazed and so taken up with the fact that there she was just smiling and speaking. If I hadn't cared a damn about her I'd have probably talked my head off.

I saw Derry a week or so later for our regular bike ride and even as he saw me coming along the road he was grinning all over his face.

'So you met her again?' he said.

'I did, I did, I did,' I almost shouted. Then Derry and I just stood grinning at each other. He was as delighted as I was but that was the great thing about Derry – he was as pleased to see his friends happy as he was to be happy himself.

This time we were off on our bikes to the Surrey hills and as we made our way down through Clapham and Croydon – still then pretty places of old houses and quiet lanes – we talked about Alice, or rather I refused to shut up about her. Derry told me to ask her to come for a cycle with us.

'But she doesn't have a bike,' I said.

'She can ride on your crossbar!'

Well it wasn't such a bad idea, but I couldn't see her agreeing to it. I spent that summer day in the Surrey hills in a state of huge excitement and afterwards could hardly remember a thing except the joy of hurtling down steep hills at a terrifying pace and sitting in a meadow to rest at lunchtime.

Disaster struck the next morning. As I accompanied the Dowager into the park I saw Alice some way ahead of us and she was with a boy. I think in my whole life I have never felt as upset and angry as I did at that moment, but the feeling luckily lasted only a moment. It was the second time I had been jealous but I quickly told myself how silly it was, for what was there to be jealous about? Alice and I had spoken twice. Had she teased me a little and in a way that suggested she might like me? Well maybe. But nothing else had happened. I also thought a little later that she must have been with someone from her work because it as an odd hour to be out socialising.

For the next couple of weeks I hovered about the street near her house on my half days off. Then for a while I stopped going on bike rides with Derry on my Sundays, but the months passed and I didn't see Alice at all. I lost weight and made more mistakes in the house and was sure everyone must have noticed how morose I was but no one ever said a word.

Then just when I least expected it Alice appeared while I was moping about in the street. The bit of anger that had been festering inside me came out in a great rush and I walked up to her and said, 'I saw you in the park, with a boy.'

Even as I said it I knew how mad I must have sounded. I felt I'd almost assaulted her.

She smiled and didn't look in the least uncomfortable.

'Was he a fair-haired boy in a white jacket?'

I couldn't reply. I looked shiftily up and down the road and nodded.

'Oh yes, that was my brother!'

I wasn't the least bit brave about this sort of thing but I had had enough of hanging around uselessly so I blurted it out.

'Would you like to come for a cycle ride? It would be with me and Derry. The three of us?'

'I don't have a bike and I can't ride one anyway,' she said and laughed.

'Don't worry. You can ride on my crossbar. Or Derry's if you prefer.'

She laughed again and reached forward and just touched my forearm very lightly and said, 'Yours is fine but we can't go far like that – I'll get a sore bum. I'm off next Sunday. Is that your day?'

It was my day so there it was: my first date. The rest of the week inevitably went by with me feeling as if I'd been drugged with the most delicious opiate available. It was like the euphoria you get from the first few drinks and no hangover to spoil it.

On the Sunday I could see the look of surprise on Derry's face when I told him I'd actually asked Alice, as he had suggested, to go for a bike ride with us and she had said yes.

'You crafty bugger!' he said. 'I never thought you'd get that far. Well done!' and he patted me on the back. Alice came along about ten minutes after that and we told her we were planning to go only as far as Kensington Gardens – to save her bum.

How exciting it was for me to be bowling along watching just inches ahead of me Alice's amazingly lovely back and her hair still tied loosely and with a faint hint of scent coming off it. I concentrated more than I had ever concentrated in my life, so terrified was I that we would fall. Imagine the humiliation of taking Alice out for the very first time and then letting her tumble into the road on her head!

We got to the park safely but my knuckles were blue from gripping the handlebars so tightly. We walked across the park to the museums in South Kensington, the three of us laughing and joking 'like millionaires', as Derry put it. It was all much easier than it might otherwise have been because Derry was there and, God bless him, he never stopped talking.

After the museums we had ice creams in the park and lay on the grass just talking. Looking back, this was one of the happiest days of my life.

Then Derry said he was going to cycle across the park and around the Round Pond, which was not allowed then – no cycling at all was allowed in the park, but Derry didn't care.

After he'd gone I lay there looking at the sky with Alice lying close by. I didn't quite dare look at her, but when I opened my eyes a few moments later her face was just above mine and she was smiling down at me.

'I think you should kiss me,' she said.

Now, having never kissed her before it was perhaps a bit mad of me but I said,

'Yes, but I'd also like you to marry me.'

She laughed and gave me what was probably a fairly quick kiss. But even with all my fumbling and inexperience it was the most exciting thing that had ever happened to me. I'm not much of a poet so it is hard to describe what it felt like but it was warm and comforting and exciting all at the same time, and such a rush to the head that I couldn't tell how much time had passed while the kiss lasted. When we stopped for a second and she smiled at me again and I could feel her breath on my face I wanted to kiss her again which I did and we only stopped when she said with a giggle, 'We've got to stop!'

'Don't you like it?'

'Of course I do, more than anything, but Derry will never come back if he sees us nibbling away at each other!'

I thought that was wonderfully funny, but then for decades after that day in the park everything Alice said made me smile, even when she was telling me off.

Ours really was quite an old-fashioned romance. And she was right about Derry. When I looked up he was coming towards us across the grass, grinning.

'I thought you'd never bloody stop!' he said.

And do you know I never kissed anyone else in the same way after that, because we did get married and I never wanted anyone else. It was almost as if by instinct Alice must have known how besotted I was.

She used to say to me later, 'I knew from that first time I saw you in the street when you stared at me with your mouth open and your eyes a couple of feet out on pea sticks that you were a safe bet and I wanted a safe bet.'

'But that means I'm not very exciting,' I said.

'Of course you are. You're exciting for me not because you climb mountains or fight duels but just because you are who you are.'

So wasn't that amazing? We knew almost nothing about each other. There was none of that upper-class business of meeting each other's parents before anything was agreed. It was only after we had properly started to see each other that I found out she was a country girl from Surrey. Her father was a publican.

'It's the smallest ruddy pub in the country,' Alice used to joke. 'If we get two customers in a day we're lucky so we keep our fingers crossed that they're drunks or we never make enough money to pay the bills!'

Chapter 24

The pub was down a small country lane near Godalming which was very remote then and I went there with Alice a few years later.

It was a pretty little pub, just as she said, tiny with the beer barrels on a rack behind the counter and two tiny bars. You could tell everything was ancient from the huge number of layers of paint on all the woodwork which gave it an odd sort of bumpy look. The pub wasn't even in the village and God knows that was small enough. No, the nearest house was three or four hundred yards away and that too was all on its own, so I wasn't surprised to hear they had so few customers. How her parents made a living at all she didn't know.

'They never made much,' she said, 'which is why I'm here in London skivvying for the rich.'

Her father was a nice enough man who shook my hand warmly. He had Alice's hair and eyes and he had the same habit she had of staring deep into you just for a moment every now and then. He seemed friendly but I sensed he was talking to me the way he might have talked to one of his customers. He also seemed oddly uninterested in Alice. I mean he wasn't excited to see her, just friendly. He didn't make a fuss or seem surprised that we'd turned up. All he said when we told him we wanted to get married was, 'That's very nice, very nice.' Then when we'd long changed the subject he suddenly said, 'That'd be pricey for you, I'd imagine, very pricey,' as if to make sure he wasn't to be expected to fund anything to do with Alice.

'Oh, he was always nice but he is the same with everyone,' she used to say about him. 'Mum says he's a good man but has no real feelings about anything except the state of his beer.'

Alice's mother didn't come down for the first half an hour we were there, which seemed very odd to me. 'She's a bit of a recluse,' laughed Alice. An hour after we had arrived and sat down to tea in the little parlour at the back of the house, I heard a steady clumping noise and moments later a very short, very dark woman with her hair in curlers and paper appeared in the doorway.

'Alice, you tearaway, why didn't you come up?' she said. She didn't wait for an answer, but said, 'And who's this?' looking at me in a way that wasn't completely friendly.

'This is Bob,' said Alice.

'I'm sure it is,' came the reply.

And that was that. She helped herself to a cup of tea and toddled off back upstairs.

Alice winked at me.

The rest of the afternoon passed quietly and then we left. Alice kissed her father and ran upstairs to kiss her mother and then we were off on the long walk back to the station.

How those two managed to produce someone as amazing as Alice still defeats me. There was something about Alice that made her unlike any of the servant girls I'd worked with and unlike any of the girls I remembered from the farms at home. You would almost say – or at least I would – that she was too good for the life she found herself in. It was as if you'd come across a private in the army who really should have been a field marshal! She had a way with her that I thought was naturally aristocratic. But then I was always biased.

We met as often as we could after that early bike ride and often with Derry who never seemed to feel in the least as if he shouldn't be there. We loved it when he came along because he was always sunny and talkative. He had a gift for drawing you out of yourself. But I used to say to him,

'I hope you don't feel out of it. Are we ever soppy when we're out?'

'I never notice you two at all,' he would reply. 'I'm far too busy enjoying the sound of my own voice and you're a great pair of listeners. And besides, you're not all over each other the whole time and we're friends, aren't we?'

And you know, we three really were the greatest of

friends in a way that I think was only really possible in those days before television. We had no distractions or entertainments other than the people we knew.

Back at work my happiness gave me huge confidence and falling in love with Alice – there, I'm not embarrassed to admit it, because that is what it was – made me think I must better myself. Being in love gave me an added incentive to get on in life. I had always wanted to, ever since those early days on the estate, but now I had an added incentive because all I wanted to do was impress Alice.

Chapter 25

It was about this time that I was given the job of looking after a young man who was staying at the Dowager's house. The Dowager didn't seem to know many young people so I was very surprised one day to be told by the butler that 'young Mr Wilkins' needed a valet during his stay.

I have no idea what Mr Wilkins's connection was to the Dowager but like most members of the upper classes in those days he had bags of self-assurance and clearly spent his days drifting from house to house, eating, drinking and talking. He had an immensely superior air – even by the standards of the time – and seemed to drift around with his nose turned up so far that his face was permanently pointing at the ceiling. I think someone at his school had clearly insisted again and again on the importance of keeping his chin up and he'd taken the advice to heart to such an extent that he had no choice now but to look down his nose at everyone. Among the other servants Mr Wilkins was known as the Bumper because he was always banging into tables and chairs and breaking vases and ornaments.

I remember the first morning I met him. I went through the usual rigmarole after knocking on his door and discreetly entering. A slight nod and then while standing meekly just inside the door I awaited instructions. If I'd been his own personal valet I would have been expected just to get on with the various things valets did and in the order in which one's master liked to have them done, but as I was, as it were, the temporary valet, I didn't know any of this. Mr Wilkins left me waiting there while he hummed a tune and wandered around his room, which was enormous. It was on the second floor overlooking the park. I gazed discreetly around as I was not at all familiar with it and, as with so many rooms in the house – pretty much all of them in fact – I was dazzled by just how much stuff they had managed to pack in. Two walls of this room were each dominated by a massive oil painting of a group of dogs. That doesn't sound remarkable. Well it didn't seem remarkable to me until I realised that the two paintings were absolutely identical.

Above the fireplace was a painting of a classical statue. In a recess to one side of the fireplace hung a large group of black silhouettes and on the other side, in another recess, a group of watercolours of mountains and lakes. Opposite and distributed round the windows were yet more dark heavy oil paintings of dogs. One showed a dog gazing hungrily at a kitten, another showed a group of dogs surrounded by dead birds. There were several small tables dotted about the room covered with silver trinkets and photographs. A square piano stood in one corner, a chaise longue in another, along with a huge walnut chest of drawers and so on.

I describe all this to give you an idea of the way these essentially Victorian houses were set up. All the rooms – even the corridors and hallways – were packed with stuff like this. One corridor had about twenty dreary busts in it as well as small pictures and full-length statues.

Perhaps the strangest thing in Mr Wilkins's room was the big stuffed fox that gazed out from its glass case on top of a chest of drawers.

After I'd waited for what had become an embarrassingly long time, Mr Wilkins finally spoke.

'John,' he drawled. 'At last. You've arrived.' He then wandered over to the window and fell silent for two minutes. Then he started again.

'My clothes are in those trunks.' He pointed vaguely. 'Along with some writing things and drawing books. Just put them all where you can. Thank you.'

And with that he drifted out of the room.

I emptied his suitcase with its beautiful wool and linen suits, his silk drawers and ties, his flannels, evening wear and a massive solid silver dressing case which I opened on top of the dressing table. All the brushes and combs and razors it contained had solid silver handles. Even I could see that the dressing case was a very beautiful thing. I'd never seen anything quite like it. I put all his suits and coats into the wardrobe in the room assuming he would ring later when he was ready to dress for dinner.

When evening came sure enough the bell rang from his room and I legged it up the stairs.

He asked me to fill a bath for him which I did, running up- and downstairs for about twenty minutes with big cans of hot water. I carefully turned my back as he began undressing. I heard him climb into the water and then he said,

'Would you mind brushing my hair? Just wet it and brush it all back straight off my head.'

I'd grown used to the odd requests people often made of servants but this was a new one. I might have been expected to hand the brushes to him and to clean them afterwards but brushing his hair was something I should think his nanny would have done!

I brushed away carefully and gently as instructed and then withdrew a few feet from the bath. He scrubbed himself and slopped the water all over the carpet so I made a note to warn the maids. He then asked me to pass his towel to him, which I did, trying all the while not to notice he was naked. He was also completely unembarrassed.

Then he said, 'That will be all, thank you.' I nodded and said, 'Very good sir,' and left the room.

I helped Mr Wilkins morning and evening over the next few days. He asked me to dry his back after one bath and to add scented oil to the water. At the time I was a little unnerved by the intimacy of all this but when I had more experience of valeting I realised it was not so unusual. I don't really think there was anything sexual about it. If you were a valet you were expected to do some very intimate things. It was just part of the job.

Mr Wilkins's visit finally came to an end and, on the last morning, without a word he gave me a pound note.

Now a pound at this time was a great deal of money and I was so delighted that it was the first thing I told Alice next time I saw her.

'He must like you!' she almost shouted, and she went on, 'I've heard that valets always get very good tips and it's a much better job than footman anyway. Why don't you try to get a position as a senior footman? But you are only allowed to try for it if the job is somewhere near here. You can't go off back to the countryside without me.'

Derry was equally adamant I shouldn't go too far.

'Don't you dare,' he said. 'We're cycling pals so you can't just up and off. There are rules about these things. And anyway every nob in London probably needs a valet.'

In the coming weeks I scoured the newspapers for likely looking advertisements. I didn't really want to try an agency unless I had to because my lack of experience as a valet might make things difficult. I thought if I could meet the person I would be valeting for I would be able to exaggerate a little about my experience and if they liked me that would be enough to outweigh my actual lack of experience. I got the sense that it was easy to learn on the job and I hadn't done so badly with Mr Wilkins. Why else would he have given me such a big tip?

Chapter 26

During the 1920s and 1930s it seemed to me that London, especially the suburbs, was completely rebuilt or built over. Every time Derry and I set off on a bike ride, whether towards Hampstead or Uxbridge, Epping or Ealing, the last fields were vanishing under bricks and mortar. It wasn't just that new houses and factories were being built; it was also that roads were widened by removing hedges and woods and houses so that old routes we'd often taken gradually became unrecognisable even to those of us who had cycled them so often.

Derry taught me to be sad about all this because he was furious that, as he put it, 'Everywhere is beginning to look the same.'

'Cheap houses and cheap roads,' he used to say. Two of our favourite pubs were demolished so that they could be replaced by much bigger, modern pubs but somehow it wasn't the same. It was all being changed to make life easier for the car and the lorry. We grumbled of course but secretly I'd have given anything to be able to buy a car. All boys and young men were mad about cars then and the passion for bicycles was fading.

About this time I received a letter from my brother saying my mother was ill so I missed seeing Alice and Derry the following Sunday when I had a whole day off. I went back to the old estate, my first visit in years.

Little had changed so far as I could see, except there were fewer horses about the place and they were trying out a new tractor or two. My mother was losing weight rapidly and looked horribly ill. I was upset that my brother had not written sooner but there was no point complaining. I sat by her bed talking to her and she was really pleased I was doing so well. I think I exaggerated a bit to cheer her up, but I had a feeling this would be the last time I saw her and I was right. A few weeks later she was dead and though my brothers stayed on the estate that was really the end of my connection with my old life.

I felt oddly divorced from everything at the funeral and wondered if I wasn't a bit of a cold fish. I wanted to get back to London and Alice and my future. In an odd way I felt completely free now that my mother and father were both dead. It was if I could only now really get on with my own life. Alice and I regularly discussed how and when we could get married but she was worried about losing her job too soon when we had hardly any money. You see, she would be asked to leave once she told the house that she had a follower, as boyfriends were called. So I continued to scour the papers for a senior and therefore higher-paid footman's job. It was to be nearly two more years before I found a job that really suited. It was not too far from Alice and paid well, but it was a job filled with far more surprises than I could have imagined.

Chapter 27

Alice wasn't in the least concerned when I told her that my new job was south of the river. I'd already shown her the advertisement in the newspaper. I almost didn't apply because it wasn't as close to Alice as I would have liked but she rightly said, 'You might never find anything just round the corner – go a bit further afield. You can get the bus up from south London when you want to see me.'

Alice didn't have a trace of jealousy in her then or later but I was a little worried that if I was further away someone else might start courting her. I was sensible enough to say this to her and she was reassuring.

'You idiot! Why would I even look at someone else? It will take me about fifty years to get bored with you and then I'll start looking around.'

So it was decided and I went off to a tall, narrow house in Kennington. Now Kennington was a really rough area back then. Most of the long lines of old terraced houses were occupied by numerous families, sometimes with several families sharing a room. Here and there a large house remained in the possession of one family and the house I stood looking up at on the day of my interview was one of those.

Long after I had retired I went back to the old house and discovered it was about two minutes from the house where Charlie Chaplin had lived in Kennington Road. Anyone who knows anything about Chaplin will know about the appalling poverty of his early life in this part of London. It was that kind of area. So I was rather nervous as I approached the building. But the wages as advertised in the paper were above what you might normally expect for a young man who had only a small amount of experience as a valet. After Mr Wilkins and his big tip I still had an idea that being a valet was a short route to easy money.

As the cab I'd taken from Regent's Park crossed the river my heart gradually sank. The blackened and mean-looking streets and alleyways of Lambeth and Kennington stretched in every direction. There were many factories along by the river which later disappeared during the bombing of London.

I'd never been south of the river before so it was an even greater shock for me to find all this misery just a few miles from the luxury of Regent's Park.

After dithering for quite some time and almost giving up and setting off back the way I'd come I thought I would at least see what they had to say for themselves in this curious-looking establishment. I looked in vain for a tradesman's entrance, so I climbed up the main steps to the door thinking, 'If this was Mayfair or Kensington I'd be kicked back down the stairs in a second but who knows what will happen here.'

I pulled a brass handle shaped like a fist. It was attached to a thin brass rod that ran up the side of the front door and disappeared into the stone lintel above the door. A distant bell sounded. Then a dog barked. Then the door opened. A middle-aged man in black opened the door right back as far as it would go into the hall and just looked at me. He had a very round face and no hair at all, not even at the sides. He didn't say a word but gave me what I can only describe as a questioning look.

'I answered your advertisement for a valet,' I said. 'Bob Sharpe. You invited me for an interview.'

'We did and you did. Come in. Would you mind waiting in here?' He had a most bizarre accent that I couldn't place, half London and half something very odd.

And as he spoke he opened a door off the hall into a small sitting room.

'You will find a seat,' he said and left very slowly and quietly, closing the door behind him.

When I describe the room as small I mean only in relation to the sitting rooms at the house in Regent's Park and the grand house in Hertfordshire. In fact the room was probably at least fifteen feet wide and twenty long. It was also very unusual in a number of ways. There was a pretty arched window at the back that looked over the garden, and inside a grand piano and a small table and sofa. Other than that, nothing. So the impression, to someone used to huge amounts of clutter in the houses of the rich, was of a room almost empty. There were a few pictures on the walls but they were extraordinary pictures that looked like nothing I had ever seen before. Gone were the usual pictures of dogs and horses, fields, hay carts and ships at sea. Instead these were pictures painted in the brightest colours imaginable of lumpy figures with no faces mangled up with blobs of random colour.

The figures in them, if indeed they were figures, were roughly outlined and painted in colours that made no attempt to imitate reality. I was astounded. I thought they must have been painted by people living in the Bedlam Hospital which was just a mile or two away. But however odd they seemed I could sense that they had been deliberately added to the room to create a specific effect which was completely at odds with the dark Victorian interiors I was used to. Here the walls were painted a pale yellow. In the hall, I noticed, they were painted a pale green. The rugs on the floor were bright and the cushions on the sofa even brighter.

I thought this was something really remarkable and I realised that the world contained a very great deal more than I had ever imagined in my limited life. It is only when I look back that I realise the simple explanation for all this: my new employer had thrown off the old world, the world I knew, and had embraced everything modern.

This was certainly confirmed when the middle-aged man with no hair returned and said, 'The master will see you now.'

My youthful bashfulness had long since vanished because so much of my work had involved dealing with people, including those with no clothes on. So this relatively modest house in Kennington held no real terrors for me. I walked along the landing behind the man in black, who was clearly some sort of butler, and then up a flight of stairs to another smaller sitting room decorated much like the first. And there sat my future employer.

At this time I'd hardly heard of Oscar Wilde but in looks and probably in manner, Mr Hall was remarkably like Wilde. He wore a long fur coat and his hair was longer than I'd seen on any adult male. He looked like one of those aristocratic little boys whose hair isn't cut till he is five years old. It was very dark brown and fell evenly with no fringe to his shoulders. Under his long fur coat he wore a fairly conventional-looking suit but with a pink cravat rather than a tie.

And then began the strangest interview of my life.

'I'm Hall,' he said. 'Delighted to meet you.' He stood up and shook my hand.

Now this was a real shock to me. Employers did not shake prospective servants' hands. As he spoke to me about my duties and I saw the room all around him I realised that this was a most unconventional man.

I could tell from his accent and manner that he was

certainly upper class, but what was he doing living in this slightly disreputable part of Kennington?

After working for him for a few years I had a pretty good idea that he must have been, in some way, the black sheep of the family. Certainly he led a very unconventional life but apart from the slight sense that you might be arrested at any time while working for him, I found he was by far the best person I ever worked for.

Chapter 28

Back at Regent's Park I packed my bags and said goodbye to the other footman and the butler, who gave me an excellent reference. He even let me look at it before putting it in its thick Manila envelope.

'Is that all right?' he asked. I said I was sure it was and he replied: 'Are you sure you don't want to read it first?'

But I was too embarrassed and only read it later. It was glowing with praise, which pleased me enormously – in fact it made my head swell a bit.

I had bought my own suits by this time so when I gave back my day suit it didn't leave me in an embarrassed position. Like most people from my background at that time I didn't own much besides my clothes. As well as my suit, a tweed coat and some flannels I had a photograph of my mother and brothers, a spare pair of black shoes, several black ties and nothing else. Not much for a man in his thirties but then I had no home of my own to put furniture and pictures in. In fact I'd never met a servant who bought furniture or knick-knacks or pictures. We expected to work in houses where you couldn't have your own things. Imagine if you'd turned up to work as a butler or valet and said, 'The lorry with my furniture will be along tomorrow.' They would have called for a psychiatrist.

I always liked to think to myself that it was all about travelling light. I made a virtue of it. It wasn't true at all but until Alice and I had somewhere of our own there was no point doing much except eat ice creams with Alice in summer and drink tea with her in winter. Furniture and pictures could wait till we were married and had somewhere to live.

On the day I left Regent's Park I took a motor taxi down through Oxford Circus and Piccadilly Circus and I remember the strange rapid click of the studs on the rubber tyres that were there to give the wheels more grip on the cobbles. Those early motor taxis seemed top heavy compared to modern cars because of course they were based on the old carriages they replaced. These were always tall to make sure the people were above the horses – true in all cases I think except, as I've said, the hansom.

We crossed the river, which still stank as there were so many factories pumping filth into it every day. I hadn't quite realised that this new job as a valet would not just involve putting out a gentleman's clothes, dusting his collar and running his bath. In many ways it was to be a job that involved some of the things I'd done as hall boy and some I was later to do as butler. As a valet you were expected to do pretty much all the personal things your master needed, from emptying the chamber pot if that's what he asked you to do to accompanying him to the opera.

Mr Hall had seemed rather vague about my duties but the money, as I've said, was very generous so within reason I didn't really mind what I was expected to do.

Something else I discovered about being a servant at this time astonished me. I was waiting in Mr Hall's bedroom about three days after I'd started work when he said, 'Now I think of it I had better buy a licence for you.'

I had never heard of this but he explained that anyone who employed a manservant in any capacity had to have a licence, one for each man. No licence was necessary for a woman servant whether she was cook, housekeeper or humble kitchen maid. The truth is that the licence system existed to ensure that only the genuine upper classes employed men. The market was controlled: if you were not a gentleman or a lady – how that was defined I'm not quite sure – you would not be issued with a licence. The idea was to keep suburban upstarts, as Derry had once described them, from getting above themselves and aping the gentry.

The licence system for male servants survived I believe until the Second World War.

Mr Hall was clearly worried about getting his licence.

'I have a licence for David' – he pronounced this *Davide* with a French accent – 'because he's been with me since my Mayfair days, but you may present a problem. You see gentlemen don't live in Kennington or even south of the river. Not since Ruskin gave up Herne Hill or whatever ghastly place he lived in. I love slumming it but the *bon ton* I'm afraid do not.'

As he said this to me in his sitting room I'm sure the look of bafflement on my face confirmed in his mind that I was a nitwit of the first order. I'd never heard of the '*bon ton*' and no one I'd worked for had ever talked to me like this. I was so astonished that I barely took in what he said.

Almost fifty years after I crossed Lambeth Bridge in the 1930s only one thing remains as it was in those far off days: the Archbishop's palace. All the rest of the low riverside buildings had gone by the 1960s.

When I arrived at the house in Kennington with my suitcases, David – the middle-aged man with no hair and a strange accent – had clearly been expecting me. He came bounding down the steps and I noticed that this time he was wearing a patch over one eye like a veteran of the Great War.

I never found out for sure, but I don't think for a minute that David was either French or a war veteran. He had what sounded vaguely like a French accent to me, though I had never been to France and had never met a French person. But once I heard him arguing with someone who had called at the house and I heard him say, 'Go on, piss off out of it!' in the accent of a cockney railway porter. He wore the eye patch for a few weeks and then it never appeared again. He also wore bow ties for a while before giving them up forever. For six months he wore a wig which he took off in the kitchen and then threw over his head like a hat when the doorbell rang or when the master's bell rang and he had to go upstairs. Sometimes he put the wig on the wrong way round or it would sit at a funny angle. The fact that it was obvious to the rest of us that he was wearing a wig didn't bother him in the slightest. Then the wig too vanished, never to be seen again.

David could be very funny and I know he thought of himself as a bit of a comedian. I once heard him going through what I later discovered was an old music hall joke with a visitor. I heard him speaking in his best French accent in the hall to a guest. The guest had asked if David had seen Mr Hall.

'I just pissed him on zer landing,' said David.

When David spoke to Mr Hall – and I was often present at these times – he would keep up the French accent but I'm sure Hall knew it was all a game because he himself would develop a hint of a French accent while talking to David.

Chapter 29

I don't think David ever really warmed to me. He'd had Mr Hall to himself for some time and I think he resented the fact that Mr Hall felt I was needed at all. But of course he couldn't show his resentment to his master so he showed it to me. He was always as superficially friendly as he was on the day he helped me lug my bags up to the fifth floor of the tall narrow house. But he remained a little distant.

When we reached the top of the house he said, 'This is your room,' and opened a door that led into a bright, clean, warm room. I thought he must have made a mistake but no this really was where I was to sleep. Like everything about Mr Hall and his house this was eccentric — not just in the sense that the room had pictures on the wall (more blobs of red and green) and a good mahogany dresser, a mirror and a fire with coal in a bucket next to it. No. It was the fact that here in Mr Hall's house the male servants — myself and David — slept at the top of the house while the maid slept in a room near the kitchen. What's more, our rooms were nothing like the usual miserable garrets given to servants. Like everything else in the house they suggested that Mr Hall was in revolt against his upper-class ancestors.

Mr Hall's maid, May, clearly had something slightly wrong with her. It was very difficult to understand what she said and she dragged one leg very slightly. She was always dropping things but Mr Hall never got angry with her. In any other house she'd have been sacked but Mr Hall would not hear of it. In fact the only time I heard him angry was when the cook told him she could not work with May. I heard Mr Hall insisting that he could not possibly do without her.

'I'm sorry, I am not prepared to discuss it,' he said and then I heard a door close and his steps coming back upstairs from the basement. The cook – who came in every day at about half past seven in the morning – was a friendly Irishwoman, but the mere presence of May changed her mood completely. I think the difficulty was that she was used to working in a certain way and May upset her notion of how things ought to be. And of course May's clumsiness made more work for the cook. On the other hand she was probably being paid far more than a cook in similar circumstances would be paid. David once mentioned that Mr Hall was a generous man and this certainly explained the wages I was being paid. Almost three pounds a week and frankly I'd have worked a twenty-hour day seven days a week for that.

I think the higher pay was partly to get people to come to Kennington and partly to keep people in a house that was definitely not run on normal lines. In fact there was nothing at all normal about the house but Mr Hall did have a curiously happy effect on the people who worked for him and indeed all those with whom he came in contact.

I remember a few weeks after I started work in Kennington I went back to Regent's Park to see Alice as I always did on my day off.

We went for tea and muffins in the Marylebone Road and I tried to entertain her by describing the oddities of my new employer. And then in a flash I felt horribly guilty. I was being very unpleasant about someone who had made my working life much easier than it had been and who was paying me a great deal more than someone with my minimal experience probably deserved.

I stopped in my tracks and ever after I was always careful to tell Alice and Derry all the gossip from Kennington when I saw them, but always to say what a marvellous person Hall was to work for. This was nothing less than the truth. It was the first time I'd ever felt anything but resentment at having to work as a servant.

Chapter 30

The routine in Mr Hall's house was chaotic, friendly and always eccentric. Cook could live out because Mr Hall rarely got out of bed or was even heard until 10 a.m., which gave her plenty of time to prepare his two eggs, tea, sliced cucumber and Bath Olivers. A Bath Oliver is a fearsomely dry biscuit.

I did absolutely nothing before 10 a.m., which was an undreamed-of luxury for me. I got up late, looked out the window, polished my shoes and read the paper. Always the paper from the day before, after Mr Hall had finished with it. At ten I boiled water for Mr Hall. I took it up to him and left it under the mirror in his dressing room. At half past ten I returned and he was back in bed but shaved. He always ate his two eggs and Bath Olivers in bed.

I would leave him for about half an hour and then collect his tray and bring him a plate of sweet biscuits that he would eat while I dressed him.

The first time I helped him get dressed I think he realised how inexperienced I was. 'It's quite simple really,' he said. 'Stockings and drawers go here, shirts and suits in there. You'll soon know which ones I want. Let's start with the green suit. I always wear the green suit on Mondays.'

I went to collect the green suit from his enormous wardrobe. When I opened the door I was faced by a line of coats and suits in a range of colours that even a woman at the time would have found garish. True, there were conventional suits too – beautiful dress suits, morning coats and the finest silk shirts. But there were also pink and green shirts, yellow trousers and even a pair of multicoloured baggy Turkish trousers that he wore occasionally late at night around the house.

I was deeply conventional and probably a bit of a prig and at first I found these strange clothes shocking. The green suit was soon found, however, and I helped him into it. All the time he talked in a quiet, slightly tense fashion and almost as if he were thinking aloud.

Once he was dressed he asked me to bring *The Times* and said, 'Try to remember how we do things. They don't change much from day to day. Actually they don't change at all.' And he laughed a quiet laugh. I noticed he had very bad teeth.

I would normally leave him with the newspaper until luncheon at one o'clock. He insisted on calling it luncheon rather than lunch – a word he hated – as did everyone of any standing in those days. Why the word lunch was so hated I will never understand.

The Dowager used to say, 'One does not know people who have lunch.'

That always prompted one of my old colleague George's impersonations back at Regent's Park. He would wander around saying under his breath, 'One does not know people who need a piss,' or 'One does not know people with two heads.'

Luncheon for Mr Hall was always white wine and a thin slice of fish cooked in a great deal of butter. He hardly ever ate meat. I would carry the fish up and he would eat alone at a round table at the back of the sitting room overlooking the garden.

I generally had a few hours off in the afternoon and was only aware now and then of what Mr Hall got up to. Occasionally there would be a visitor but I'd been told not to answer the door. Afternoon was David's time to open the door. I did it only until lunchtime. This was a rule I never really understood, unless it was just to give David something to do, because, so far as I could see, he did almost nothing the rest of the time.

I lit the fires and kept them going. I carried the meals up and the plates down, and I helped the master to get dressed and undressed.

Occasionally Mr Hall went out in the afternoon straight after luncheon, called his own cab and didn't come back till evening or occasionally not at all till the next day.

David said, 'Do not worry. If 'ee 'as fallen in zer river we will find out soon enough.'

Supper at around seven would consist of more fish or occasionally a piece of almost raw steak and a few almost raw vegetables. And always thin delicate-looking wines, mostly German. Sometimes he would ask for wine with his eggs in the morning but I never saw him drunk in the daytime. Night was a different matter.

Chapter 31

Mr Hall didn't own his own motor car. Horse-drawn carriages were all disappearing from London now at an extraordinary rate. Only a few milkmen still used them and the rag-and-bone men and a few chimney sweeps. The rich wanted the new motor cars. By the mid 1930s they were everywhere and the well-to-do had got round the problem of being terrified of driving by employing chauffeurs. But Mr Hall had neither car nor carriage. He liked to take cabs and he liked best of all to take them to the theatre. I sat outside various West End theatres on many occasions while he watched mostly Noël Coward and Somerset Maugham plays which seemed to be on everywhere in the 1930s. They were always hugely successful so far as I could see and Mr Hall loved them, but they were considered a little scandalous I think by older people.

Then one night as I sat in the cab which he paid to wait two hours, Mr Hall appeared, smiled at me as he climbed into his seat and said, 'Next time I think you should come.' I put the rug over his lap, reminded the driver of our address in Kennington and off we went. It was only then as we trundled through the busy streets that I realised he meant I should accompany him not just to the theatre as I always did anyway but *into* the theatre.

I said, 'Yes of course, sir,' worried that I would feel out of place. But what could I say? Servants simply did what they were asked or told to do.

It was shortly after this and a few days before my first ever visit to the theatre that I began to think I would probably have to start looking around for another job. It was midsummer and very warm. I was in my shirtsleeves reading the paper in my room. I realised it was time to lay the table for luncheon so began to make my way downstairs. Each landing of the staircase had a tall window that looked out onto the garden and as I passed the window on the second landing I glanced down into the small garden. There, sitting on a deckchair and smoking away, was Mr Hall in a straw hat and absolutely nothing else. He was completely naked, very thin and white. And, unfortunately for me, he had a bell.

'Is he going to stay in the garden like that for long?' I asked David.

'Why? Do you object?' said David. 'He loves the sun. It's simple. I believe he models himself on Mr William Blake who used to sit naked in his Lambeth garden all year round. He thinks that if Blake can do it so can he.'

I had never heard of William Blake and assumed it

was one of Mr Hall's friends. I felt a terrible fool when I found out Blake was a poet who had been dead for over a century.

'Is he going to ring the bell for me?' I asked.

'Of course,' said David. 'Don't worry about it. He will ring, you go out and look him straight in the eyes and he will ask for a glass of wine or whatever. Same as always. Easy.'

About twenty minutes later I heard the bell. Down I went and out into the garden. Mr Hall looked up, smiled just a little, and said:

'Would you bring me a tray with biscuits and a glass of hock. The sweet biscuits.'

I nodded, turned, and went back into the house. It wasn't shocking as long as you were very careful where you looked. I think Mr Hall enjoyed the fact that I was a little uncomfortable but since he was such a good boss in so many other ways it was difficult to be really offended. But the prude in me kept saying, 'You have to leave. What if anyone finds out? What will people think?' You can't imagine how truly shocking that sort of thing was at that time – a time when people hated even using the word 'leg' in women's company!

When I returned with the biscuits and wine Mr Hall asked me to lay out his blue suit.

'We're going to the theatre,' he announced.

I bowed slightly and said, 'Yes indeed, sir.'

'No, I mean we are going together.'

I nodded and retreated, hoping he would remember to put his trousers on before we set off.

Chapter 32

I'd been enjoying my time with Mr Hall because, as I say, we servants – David, myself, the maid and the cook – had very little to do compared with a job in a bigger house where there were more family members and regular visitors. But what with his eccentricities and now this sunbathing I realised there was a downside to it. I don't know why I found it so difficult to be asked to wait on him while he had no clothes on but I did. I think looking back that it was partly my narrow country upbringing, partly I suspect because most people would have hated it at the time as people hated to do or say anything that attracted attention or made them look anything out of the ordinary. Certainly I wasn't brave enough to go against the fashion. I think I judged Mr Hall rather harshly, which I regretted later on.

But that night we went to the theatre with a properly attired Mr Hall and watched a play by Noël Coward. Mr Hall hardly said a word to me until afterwards. At the theatre door he asked, 'Did you enjoy it?' and before I could answer said, 'Would you get a cab and wait for me in it?' Then he turned on his heel and disappeared. I saw him walk up a narrow alley-way at the side of the theatre and through a narrow door. He was clearly going backstage to meet the actors.

I loved that play. It was called *Red Pepper* and I seem to recall that the playwright was one of the actors. This was the first time I had really seen how the other half lived when they were relaxing. I had been to the cinema a few times with Alice and Derry but this seemed infinitely more glamorous.

Mr Hall took me to the theatre on several other occasions during my years with him and we saw Charles Hawtrey and Laurence Olivier, but much as I enjoyed it all I realised that it was not really for the likes of me. We sat in the most expensive seats and I was convinced that other people nearby could tell that I was not one of them, that I was a servant. From that point of view it was all slightly uncomfortable. I was of course silly and should have realised that Mr Hall was trying to be different as he was to some extent in every area of his life. I'm sure he enjoyed the revolutionary idea of taking his valet to the theatre. It was all part of his need to throw over the old world inherited from the Victorians. I think he really hated doing anything conventional at all.

In my old age I could look back and admire Mr Hall in a way that was impossible at the time. Then I was constantly worried that he would do something outrageous. It wasn't so bad if he did mad things in the house where only the servants were aware what was going on, but there was always the risk that he would do something in public, and even to be seen with him in his brightly coloured evening wear was alarming and made people stare. But I will always be grateful that he took me to the theatre and treated me so well.

Best of all he allowed me to work both as his valet and as his butler which would stand me in good stead in future.

I was earning enough now to save a major part of my wages. Alice loved my stories of life in Kennington but I was careful now not to mock Mr Hall. I just concentrated on the fact that I was being paid well and that we might be able to marry soon. Alice never seemed to change. She was always her sunny easy self and the only comment she made about Mr Hall was that he sounded much nicer than her employers.

'They own a coal mine,' she used to say, 'but they hate the idea of anyone knowing that's how they get their money!'

My most vivid memory of Mr Hall was of the time he was nearly arrested while I waited for him outside a public lavatory. I knew enough about the world by then to realise that Hall was homosexual but I found it very difficult to mind much and in those days you were meant to mind a great deal.

When the policeman appeared out of nowhere and approached Mr Hall I immediately went over to them.

The policeman had his notebook in his hand and was looking very stern. Mr Hall was pale but oddly animated. I could see his eyes glittering in the dark and he was smiling very slightly. He put his hand up as I approached as if to indicate I was to say nothing.

Then began the most extraordinary performance. I have never forgotten it. Hall began to talk to the policeman in a quiet way and within minutes they were laughing and joking together. After perhaps five minutes Hall had given the policeman his card, the notebook had been put away and the policeman tipped his helmet and walked off. On two or three occasions after that I saw the policeman in his civvies at Hall's house. I cannot remember exactly what Hall said but it would have charmed a corpse back to life. It was impossible not to admire what Hall had been able to do, but I couldn't help feeling sad that someone less well educated, less obviously upper class, would not have fared so well under similar circumstances. And this was at a time when you could still get two years' hard labour in Pentonville for doing what Hall had done.

Chapter 33

As everyone knows, the 1930s were economically a bad time in England. You saw poverty everywhere and tens of thousands working in industry, especially the docks, were thrown out of work. I think the very rich were barely affected by the Depression and the aftermath of the First World War. Many of them escaped the worst effects of those terrible years, which lasted until the late 1930s and then became even worse during the Second World War – except of course for the fact that unemployment eased as all the young men were called up.

The rich probably *felt* that were having a terrible time of course. Fewer had footmen and maybe they had to pay higher taxes, but the very rich could afford to lose some of their servants and some of their investments because they started off with so many and so much anyway. If you lose a third of a huge fortune, you still have a huge fortune – that's how I looked at it – and although servants of all kinds became harder to get in the 1930s it wasn't just because the rich could no longer afford to employ them.

It was also because the people who had once been happy to work as domestics were sick and tired of it. They wanted to work in factories, which had become cleaner and safer than they'd been before the Great War.

Mr Hall showed no signs of financial problems and so I never felt I might suddenly find myself out of a job and with no money. I just carried on because that was all I could do.

Mr Hall seemed to lead a life that was entirely separate from the way other people lived. No relatives called at the house and few friends. But he did have occasional parties and as I was doing more of the butler's work now, these took me further out of the narrow little world that I had so long inhabited. The one I remember most involved me meeting someone who later became quite famous.

The preparations for the party began about two days before it was due to take place. They began when the yellow drawing-room curtains were taken down by David and replaced by deep red curtains.

'What on earth is the point of that?' I asked.

'I have no idea,' said David. 'Yellow is too bright for a party I should imagine. To create the right atmosphere it needs to be darker.' He laughed. Champagne boxes began to arrive, which struck me as odd as Mr Hall only drank hock and other German wines.

When I took Mr Hall his morning tray the day after the champagne arrived he said,

'I'm going to have a little party tomorrow night.

Just a few friends. Keep them well supplied with wine, would you?' And that was that. I had to rely on David to discover what time the proceedings would start and what I should do.

At eight o'clock the following evening I began answering the door to a string of very odd-looking people. There were several girls with shingled hair – that strange short crimped style that had started in the 1920s and was still fashionable – and at least a dozen men dressed pretty much as Mr Hall dressed, in plum-coloured suits or pale green. One man came in very conventional evening wear but had a woman's cloche hat on his head. Another turned up in a purple cape that reached to the ground. Half the time when I put my hands out to take their coats and gloves I had no idea what I would be given. Some had no gloves at all and some no hats, which was very rare then. The man with the cloak kept his cloak on and several people handed me their jackets which they might have been expected to keep on. Several of the men appeared to be wearing make-up and as soon as they entered the drawing room they started a shrill intense conversation that lasted from the moment they arrived till the moment, at about six o'clock the next morning, when the last guest left. Along with David I stayed up all night carrying trays of drinks. No one seemed the least interested in eating and there was no food. On hearing there was to be a party, Cook had vanished an hour earlier than usual with a tight-lipped look of disgust on her face.

I noticed too that some of the guests had rough London accents while others spoke in the most refined way – accents that would have put the Dowager in Regent's Park to shame. It was like a fancy-dress party where everyone is actually wearing their own clothes.

One very thin young man put his hand on my arm as I went round with the drinks at about midnight and said, 'You're very good. Why don't you come with me?'

I thought he meant why didn't I come and work for him so I said, 'I'm so sorry but I am engaged already to work for Mr Hall.' He must have thought me a terrific fool because it was obvious I worked for Mr Hall. Why else would I be there? Perhaps he thought that I was just playing at being the valet as they were all playing at being exotic birds of every kind.

The young man said, 'Engaged. You lucky thing,' and wandered off.

I mentioned this encounter to David who said, 'That was Mr Crisp. Mr Quentin Crisp.'

The name meant nothing to me, but many years later I recognised his picture in the newspapers. By then all Mr Hall's friends might have been famous, if only for their bizarre dress sense! And by then Hall was dead. I left a forwarding address when I eventually left Kennington and David wrote to tell me in 1942 that Mr Hall was in hospital and was not expected home again – that was his way of putting it.

I don't know why he wrote to me. Perhaps he simply contacted anyone who was listed in the address book. I replied saying how sorry I was but I never heard from him again.

One of my favourite memories of Mr Hall was his insistence on certain days of changing his clothes almost continually. Normally he didn't bother even to dress for dinner, but now and then I would get him dressed at 9 a.m. for breakfast; then I would help him change at 11 a.m. for church; then he would return and I would help him dress for lunch. At 5 p.m. he would change his clothes, again with my help, for tea and then at 8 p.m. he would change for dinner. At 11 p.m. he would change for bed.

When I say he would change I really mean change. Everything except his underwear would come off and he was meticulous about which suit and waistcoat were to be worn for each event of the day.

Changing this often was absolutely standard every day among the upper classes and valets were there to make sure it all went smoothly, and this made some sense in big houses where there were large families and visitors. But why Mr Hall did it at all is a mystery because most days he had his breakfast, luncheon, tea and dinner alone.

One of my last outings with Mr Hall was to church. We went to one of those big dull Victorian warehouse churches somewhere in Kennington and I carried Mr Hall's prayer book in for him, although he never asked for it. As the service progressed I looked across at him and noticed how moved he seemed. This was also one of the few times I saw him dressed completely conventionally.

But I had decided to leave. My decision wasn't based entirely on my priggishness although that was certainly part of it. The real reason was that I knew the time had come to realise my ambition and apply for a job as a proper butler. When I explained this to Mr Hall he offered to increase my wages if I would stay but I told him – and it was not far from the truth – that I had grown up in the countryside and wanted to go back, especially if I could get a situation as a butler proper.

He was very good about it and gave me a reference that I probably didn't deserve and I will always be grateful to him for that. The reference said I had carried out the duties of butler and valet meticulously and was well qualified to take on the role of butler in any household.

Chapter 34

Alice and I decided to marry in 1937. People said war was coming but until the last minute most of us thought that it just couldn't happen. The politicians were bound to sort something out. We believed them when they waved their bits of paper. But our decision to get married had nothing to do with war coming or not coming. We decided to get married because we were fed up waiting and at last we'd saved what I thought was enough money. Our courting had lasted more than ten years, which probably sounds insanely long to young people, but we didn't want to be living in a single room somewhere with no money and we knew that Alice would be sacked before time if we rushed things. We'd seen each other almost every week in that time and although I can recommend long engagements, there are limits!

For one thing you get to know each other really well, as we did, by the time you take the plunge and live in the same house together. We'd had two holidays, in each case to boarding houses at the seaside, once to Weymouth and once to Margate. We were very nervous that they would somehow sense we were not married but I don't think the landlady cared a bit in either case. They were just pleased to have someone staying – and paying.

As well as having enough money we knew by now that more and more houses were employing staff who lived out. Employers had no choice because people were less prepared to give up all their time to their employers and there was a shortage of staff. We wanted to find someone who would provide a cottage on an estate or a separate flat in a big house but it was that or nothing.

Alice had had enough of London too. We decided to try to get work in a county I knew – Hertfordshire. It was close to London which suited us because we hated the idea of some remote house in Herefordshire or Shropshire where we would feel completely isolated.

I tried the newspapers, which was the usual route to a new job, but was advised by David that an agency would be better. Mr Hall was quite happy to keep me on until I had found a position that suited me.

'And I don't mind a bit,' he said, 'if you change your mind.'

I still tried the newspapers but they seemed to be filled with jobs in Norfolk and Lincolnshire so I gave up and took David's advice. On my afternoon off I set off for a London staff agency. They had several jobs for butlers in Hertfordshire, Essex and Bedfordshire – all of which we would have tried – but in each case they wanted far more experience than I had or could pretend to have.

The plan was that, if I could get a job as a butler in the countryside with living quarters, Alice and I would marry and off we would go. It wasn't going to be easy, but with my excellent references under my arm I was confident. The difficulty was my lack of real experience.

I kept a wary eye on the newspapers while waiting for the agency to contact me. Then, when I was least expecting it, I found something that really looked as if it might suit.

I wrote immediately to a Mr Clark who lived in a house near Berkhamsted. He replied by return saying that he would be delighted to see me for an interview and I assumed, since I told him in my letter I was about to be married, that he would take account of the fact.

Mr Hall kindly allowed me to take a day off and I caught the train to Berkhamsted where Mr Clark himself met me. How times had changed. The idea that the Dowager would meet a servant at the station – or anywhere – would have been unthinkable. Yet here was this old-fashioned-looking man in a strange-looking woollen suit that must have been very uncomfortable on this warm day. I was astonished that he should come himself to meet me but like so many members of the upper classes he was an amazing mix of eccentric and deeply conventional.

He had long ago dispensed with footmen he told me but his wife still had her lady's maid and there were a cook and a housemaid. But that was all. He wanted to keep them all on a tight rein he said, and he said it as if he had decided I was already working for him.

'Cook can be rather difficult so we must keep her on a tight rein,' he said again and then ten minutes later, 'The maid is a confounded cretin as are all maids so she must be kept on a tight rein.'

I sensed he was quite a character because apart from repeating himself he drove his huge car – a Hispano-Suiza – almost into the ditch on several occasions because he insisted on looking out the windows and commenting on the quality or otherwise of cows leaning over hedges, birds flying by, crops, streams and passing cars. He also insisted that I sit in the back as if I were the master and he the man!

His house was half an hour or thereabouts by car from the town and in what seemed a remarkably remote area given that we were relatively close to London. It was a big, rather run-down-looking house, part brick, part stone, and looked like it had been built at quite different times and in completely unrelated styles.

'It's a bloody mess,' said Mr Clark as we drove up

the drive. He drove round the back of the house and dropped me at the servants' door.

'Don't want the others to get silly ideas,' he said as he drove off and back to the front of the house. I knocked on the back door and waited and a moment later Mr Clark reappeared, peering out from the back door at me. He led me in and through the usual maze of passages till we reached a drawing room that looked down to a lake at the side of the house.

'Do take a seat,' he said.

I looked around nervously and he indicated a chair at the side of a big brown desk piled high with papers. He took the seat on the other side of the desk and gazed at the floor.

I was braver now than I would ever have been at any time in the past and I was quite honest with him about the fact that I had previously worked as a valet-butler rather than as a butler proper. But he didn't seem to mind in the least. He simply asked if I would be able to clean silver, wait at table, organise the fires and the other staff and so on. He also asked if I minded doing some of the jobs a footman would formerly have done. I didn't mind at all. The salary was £200 a year which was good. But when I explained that I would like to live out and that I was to be married shortly he seemed rather put out even though I had mentioned all this in my letters.

He looked back down at the carpet and after a while said, 'Never mind, I'm sure we can find a solution to this. There is a cottage in the garden.' And that was that. He drove me back to the station, shook hands and off I went. He told me I should start in 'about a month'.

'Summer,' he said. 'Just the ticket.'

I disappeared into the station. How things had changed. There he was shaking my hand, driving me in his own car and taking my views into consideration. This was how far the servant world had come. I might have needed a job but he also needed a butler and butlers were now harder than ever to come by.

I mentioned that Mr Clark was an eccentric, which is true, but his eccentricities were very different from those of Mr Hall, as I was soon to discover.

Back in London I told Alice the good news. I boasted that I had insisted I could not take the job if married quarters were not available and that Mr Clark had immediately come up with a solution. I made myself the hero of the hour.

My work day would still be rather long – seven in the morning until dinner had finished in the evening – but that was to be expected. I was also required to look after the wine cellar, which I had been told contained several thousand bottles of wine, some dating back to the middle of the nineteenth century. There was a wine book where each bottle bought and consumed was logged, but this again was perfectly standard procedure.

I was also in charge of the silver, which had to be

polished by me each week. It was kept in the butler's pantry where, only a few years earlier, I would have been expected to sleep. Wasn't it wonderful that, for me at least, those days were over? The old idea that the butler should defend the family silver with his life now seemed almost comic.

I knew I would have to manage the other staff but it was not a big household and most of the work was simply to keep an account book of their wages and hiring and firing. Luckily, in the ten years and more that I worked for Mr Clark no one left and no one started work: his cook and his maid were from the local village and had no desire to move. But all these duties were peripheral. My main job as butler was, of course, to wait at table and, as we used to say, to look the part.

Day-to-day activities for a butler can be very dull indeed because the routine of cleaning and polishing and serving dinner hardly changes. Unless you have a boss like Mr Clark, who was full of surprises, you end up longing for some disaster – a fire in a bedroom, the collapse of a wall, an explosion in the grounds – just to have something new to think about. In the country-side round Berkhamsted nothing much seemed to have happened for centuries and the only adventures and excitements stemmed from Mr Clark himself. He was very much like the sort of person I remembered from the estate where I was born in the sense that his only interests were shooting and hunting. On the day of my interview I had seen only one side of him, the civilised if slightly stiff side, but he was actually a very split sort of man. A strange mixture of reasonableness and blind fury. He was like a toddler, all smiles one minute, rages the next.

Chapter 35

Just weeks before we moved to Berkhamsted Alice and I were married. Derry was best man and we were married at Caxton Hall, just a few minutes' walk from Victoria Station. We had a wedding breakfast for our few friends which was an old-fashioned thing to do even then but it was what Alice wanted. I can still remember how she smiled at me all day and I never tired of looking at her. Even in old age I thought she was lovely, partly because she really was very pretty but also because of the sense of calm that almost always hovered about her. She used to get cross with me sometimes of course and I got cross with her but our great secret was to forget all about any little disagreements as fast as possible.

Alice and I were such old friends by the time we married that being wed made little difference except for the fact that we could now live together, a very difficult thing to do back then if you were not married – unless you were an aristocrat. There was undoubtedly one rule for the rich and one for the poor in this respect. A woman who was known to have had sex with someone she wasn't married to would certainly be sacked if she worked in domestic service. But I remember George telling me back at the Dowager's house in Regent's Park that when he had first started work there the older staff still talked about the excitement that had occurred in 1900 when Catherine Walters, Edward VII's mistress, had called to see the Dowager for tea.

The staff would have spat at one of their own who had slept with as many men as Walters, who was known as Skittles. But of course she was famous and a royal courtesan so she could do no wrong in anyone's eyes, rich or poor, aristocratic or common.

She was a celebrity and that was enough. 'But she's only famous for sleeping with people,' said George. 'I could be famous for that!' George told me that, having been complimented by a gentleman for her rosy complexion after a long ride in the park, Skittles replied, 'That's nothing. You should see my ruddy arse!'

Derry saw us to the station when the great day came for us to leave London and we promised to keep in touch. He looked very gloomy about us going. We three had been friends for such a long time so it was a wrench, but what could we do? We put our trunks on the train and waved goodbye from the windows. I remember as if it were yesterday, the smell of coal smoke and steam all round. I remember the blackened walls of the backs of houses as the train made its way up the long slow incline through north London and out into the countryside and at last to Berkhamsted. We took a taxicab from the station to our new home. It was a small brick cottage and as it turned out it was one of two owned by Mr Clark. The other was kept permanently empty for some reason I never discovered.

Our cottage was rather damp and the rooms were small with low ceilings but it had three rooms upstairs, a boiler or copper for heating water and a modern range. Best of all it looked out on to the road and away from the main house, which was rather too close for comfort in some ways. In those days motor traffic wasn't so bad that the road running under the window was a problem. In fact it seemed more of an advantage than anything because most people were still in love with cars and enjoyed seeing them go past. I worried that Alice would be bored and in the first few weeks in the house I think I rather nagged her about this.

'Now look here, Mister Bob,' she said. 'I will tell you when I get bored or you will know because I will start throwing the cups and saucers around!'

When I pointed out that we still had hardly any crockery, she just laughed. In our first few months at the new house life was not all sweetness and light. The cottage had only basic furniture but Alice gradually filled it with very beautiful odds and ends that she found on her once-weekly visits by bus to the town.

'You'd live any old where,' she said to me, and this

was true to some extent. I had never thought about making a house comfortable for myself because I had always lived in rooms in other people's houses. Alice had only lived in other people's houses too, but she had a natural gift, I think, for home-making as I suppose it is called. With hardly any money she made our little cottage look lovely. Perhaps this was because she had worked as a housemaid for so long and was used to arranging things in the best way. She found chairs and pictures at farm sales, as well as flower pots and ornaments. She worked occasionally at the house when the maid was off or there was an emergency but I was rather old-fashioned and preferred it when she was at home.

We had left it rather late to have children but our daughter Marjorie was born in 1941, a few years after we'd left London. We always considered ourselves incredibly lucky to have left before the Blitz and to have had a child at all.

I had hardly noticed the First World War but there was no escaping the horrors of the Second, with the villages round about filled with children from London. At night I was sure I could hear the distant bombing over London although it was more than thirty miles away. The trains became impossible and there was little or no petrol for Mr Clark's car so for the duration we were rather stuck in our rural hideaway – all of us, including the rich. Travel except on foot or by bus now and then was very difficult. The trains were almost all being used for troops and armaments and if you did manage to catch a train the chances are it would take a day to do a journey that should have taken two hours.

But keeping Mr Clark at home was perhaps no bad thing.

Chapter 36

My first experience of Mr Clark's slightly dotty nature occurred when he went shooting. I had told him in my interview that, as a boy, I had worked with my gamekeeper father and was used to handling shot-guns. This was always something that pleased prospective employers because I think they felt it meant you had upper-class rather than middle-class connections – ridiculous perhaps, but shooting and fishing were still seen as aristocratic sports. If I'd said I'd accompanied my former boss to play golf I'd have been shown the door!

So Mr Clark was delighted about my sporting background, such as it was, and clearly recalled this when he asked me to accompany him on a day's shoot a few months after Alice and I joined him. I imagined this would be the sort of formal pheasant shoot that I remembered from my childhood. As it turned out, it was nothing of the sort.

We climbed into Mr Clark's old-fashioned and rather dilapidated Hispano-Suiza with half a dozen shotguns and a massive rifle. None was cased so they would be on view to anyone who looked through the car windows. There was nothing really odd about this as I had regularly seen people carrying shotguns in public, even on London buses. No one was the least bothered. People who liked shooting would get the bus out to the suburbs where they might have permission to shoot over a few fields. One chap I knew took the bus every Saturday to a golf course in Pinner to help keep the rabbits down. But despite the fact that guns were a familiar sight, there was something about carrying this armoury in the car that made me nervous, particularly as we had with us what looked horribly like a large-bore Victorian elephant gun!

We drove along a quiet back road and eventually stopped at the edge of a wood about half a mile from the house. To this day I am certain that the wood was not owned by Mr Clark.

'Come on,' said Mr Clark. 'Bring Big Bertha and that 12-bore.' He pointed to a rather lovely old gun with Damascus barrels and great big hammers like spaniels' ears. Damascus barrels have long vanished from shotguns – they had a very distinct and very beautiful colour that resulted from the peculiar way they were made.

Then when I had shouldered the two guns, he changed his mind and said, 'Oh bother, bring that one too,' and again he pointed to one of the shotguns.

'Yes, bring the Boss,' he said. The Boss was a

beautiful side-by-side shotgun and it didn't get its name for any sinister reason. It was made by Boss & Co., one of the famous makers of the day.

I carried the three heavy guns wearing my dark formal butler's suit which frankly made me look ridiculous, but Mr Clark had insisted on it when I asked him what I should wear. I had long ago thrown out my own shooting suit anyway, so perhaps it was just as well.

Mr Clark's own clothes were not much better. He was wearing the same suit he'd been wearing when he met me at the station. I discovered from the cook that it was what was called a Jaeger suit. It was woollen and had very narrow trousers and a tight-fitting jacket that buttoned right up to the throat. It was very strange-looking and had not been in fashion since around 1900 I think and then only among bohemian artists and writers, never among country gentlemen. Mr Clark was always going on about this suit. 'It's hygienic you see because the wool is undyed,' he had told me early on. 'Very important that. If it was dyed it wouldn't work at all but as it is it draws out the poisons. Do you see? We're all full of dreadful poisons and the wool gets them out of the system and keeps you warm at the same time. Hardly need to wash when you're wearing this – undyed wool next to the skin. Perfect.'

'Indeed sir,' I replied, thinking, 'Oh how I wish you would wash!' Because if there was one thing about Mr Clark that everyone noticed it was that he positively hummed. He smelled like a Labrador that had spent the night in a muddy ditch. Now most people were a bit smellier in those days than they were later on when everyone or almost everyone had baths. In those days only the well-off bathed every day, but Mr Clark didn't bathe at all because of that damned suit. In fact he had several of these suits and wore them turn and turn about.

So there we were, poaching someone else's wood with Mr Clark dressed in what looked like a music-hall comedian's crazy suit, and me clumping along behind him dressed in a black butler's suit while carrying three guns and a heavy leather cartridge bag.

From the moment we entered the wood Mr Clark pretty much fired at anything and everything that moved. Sometimes he would fire if he heard a bit of rustling in the undergrowth or he would take ridiculously long – and very unsporting – shots at pigeon, magpies and anything else flying overhead or perching in a tree. I say his shots were unsporting because they were at too great a range and he had almost no chance of cleanly killing any of the birds he fired at. But I could not say a word because it was not my place to do so. It would look like criticism. Inwardly I was horrified.

After a time, perhaps half an hour, he handed the shotgun to me and began loading the rifle, which I think was a .308 – a massive bore for anything we were likely to encounter in an English wood.

'There are some very good fallow deer here,' he whispered to me.

'I'm sure there are,' I replied, but I knew from the noise we were making as we wandered along that any deer within half a mile of us had long since departed. After a short while he crouched down and urgently waved at me to get down. He crawled on his stomach for about ten feet with me crawling behind carrying the other guns. He stopped. He pushed the gun through some bracken and after a pause he fired. The report was shockingly loud. Like a blast of dynamite followed by a series of echoes.

'That'll teach them,' he said. 'She's a powerful beast. Very powerful,' he muttered, looking admiringly down at the .308. And with that he stood up and marched back to the car. God knows what he had fired at. I suspect he simply fired into the undergrowth.

It was a relief to get back to the house, but even in the house there were tensions as there always are in houses where there are servants. The maid from the village had an odd accent and there was something about her that caught my attention, so one day I stopped her and asked where she was from. She told me her story. Her father was a professor, she said, at a university in Germany and she had been training to be a teacher. I asked why on earth she was working as maid in England.

She said, 'I am a German Jew. It was very hard for us. I could not stay. It was terrible. We were spat at in the streets and sometimes knocked down. It was terrible, terrible. Some of us were killed. So my parents got me a job here in England.'

This was a great shock to me because, like most people in England, I knew little about what went on in other countries and I always remembered Esther, the maid, in later years after the news about Auschwitz and other camps became more widely known. Despite her middle-class background she was extremely hardworking and never complained. I have never forgotten her.

Chapter 37

I stayed with Mr Clark until long after the war ended and as soon as petrol was more generally available he began to drive again. The Hispano-Suiza was now mouldering slowly in a shed and he bought a gleaming black 1930s Wolsey. He had more or less given up shooting by now and instead he insisted we go out several days a week in the car to try to run down pheasants and deer. He was remarkably successful at it.

'It's perfectly sporting,' he would say, 'so long as we do it in season. And with the price of meat it's our national duty.'

The front of the car never had any working lights because they were smashed by the birds and animals he hit, but he was scrupulous about stopping and picking up the carcases. If he hit a deer he would take out his hip flask and offer me a nip, he was so delighted. We sat together in the front of the car always. This was partly because he liked to talk while driving and partly because the back seats were in a terrible state. At some stage in the past he had allowed his dogs to travel in the back and they had ripped out all the stuffing. This didn't bother him in the slightest even though the interior was ruined. The car also constantly stank of dead deer and rotting pheasants. Once again, you saw how things had changed. I sat in the front seat of the car with him on these outings and was allowed to drink from his flask. It was partly eccentricity of course but also partly the fact that the old rules were weakening. Can you imagine the old Dowager sharing a flask with me? She'd rather have been hanged, drawn and quartered I should say. Even Mr Hall, lovely man though he was, would not have been that familiar with me.

Up at the house most of the old rules did still apply, though I felt we were all play-acting a little. The rigidity had somehow leaked out of the system and employers were more wary of treating their servants in a way that looked too high-handed. Isn't it funny how fashion and social attitudes changed so much in my lifetime?

They didn't change in every respect, however. Like all the people I'd worked for Mr Clark felt no embarrassment in front of me. He would do things with me watching that he would never have done with someone from his own background.

When his niece came to stay, life for me at least turned into a bit of a nightmare because he would try to paw his niece's daughter whenever her mother was out of the room. The girl was very beautiful but like most teenagers baffled by adults. Mr Clark took advantage of her. What made the situation really strange is that the girl did not seem to mind. She would sit on the sofa reading a book while he pushed his hand along her thigh or he would put his arm around her and allow his hand to rest on her chest. He always removed his hands quickly when he heard the door open but he had no qualms at all about doing it in front of me. Perhaps the daughter didn't realise the significance of what was going on.

At dinner he would always sit next to the daughter and I could always tell when he started to touch her leg under the table because she would turn and smile at him. There might be half a dozen or more of them at dinner including the girl's mother and the conversation would carry on as if nothing was happening.

I saw this happen often at dinner but it also happened in the drawing room after dinner. The girl would come in and pick up a magazine and sit quietly in a corner to read it. If Mr Clark came in he would always go straight over to her. He would sit by her on the sofa and immediately put his hand on her leg. She would carry on reading, yawn and lie back. He would carry on in the same slightly mechanical way. Only once do I recall hearing her object. She said, 'Please no, please!' and made a half-hearted effort to push him off. It was impossible for me to intervene even when he forced his hand up her skirt. He would just laugh and pull her on to his lap. He would then let her go and she would slowly leave the room.

Things came to a head one morning when I saw her walking down the drive on her own with a fixed and very grim look on her face and with no luggage. I reached the house and heard her mother shouting at Mr Clark. I didn't quite catch what was said but as I stood in the hall Mr Clark came out of the drawing room and said, as calm as you like, 'Would you get my niece's things ready? She is leaving.'

He didn't look in the least put out or discomfited and as he walked towards the stairs he smiled at his wife who had come out to hear what all the fuss was about. She smiled back and accompanied him upstairs and that was the end of it, though in the rest of my time with Mr Clark I never saw his niece or her daughter again.

Mrs Clark was perhaps the oddest creature in the house because she never seemed to know what was going on. She kept two cows supposedly for milk but in fact they were her pets and her constant companions. Every morning she would get up at five o'clock to milk them into a series of buckets. She then took the milk to the kitchen where she left the buckets until the cream had settled on the top. Cook was under strict instructions never to touch the milk because once it had cooled and the thick cream had settled Mrs Clark would come back down and sit for an hour carefully skimming the cream off using a metal dish.

She talked to the cows for hours, but she never

talked to her husband so far as I ever heard. They seemed to get on well enough, perhaps because they had so little to do with each other! Certainly they slept in separate rooms – not just separate but in different parts of the house well away from each other.

They would usually meet at dinner but unless there were visitors a whole meal might pass in silence except for Mr Clark asking me occasionally for more wine or initiating strange conversations about the wine or his trousers or his neighbours.

He would say, 'Walker has been told to turn the gravel. Why doesn't he turn it?' It was not my place to answer and his wife would say nothing so there was an uncomfortable silence.

Sometimes he would look at me directly as I stood against the back wall of the dining room and say, 'This is a very intelligent burgundy, Mr Sharpe. Very intelligent.' I would nod discreetly and say, 'It is indeed, sir.' He would then say, 'What do you think of it, my dear?' looking at his wife. She would completely ignore the remark and they would both fall into a long silence. Months would pass with evenings spent like this and with dinner finished Mr Clark would retreat to his part of the house while Mrs Clark would go out to say goodnight to her cows.

The dining room had heavy damask curtains that were beaten once a week by a woman from the village but never really cleaned properly. The ceiling had long cracks across it and the thick rugs were worn here and there so the threads could be seen, and below stairs we would occasionally hear a thump as Mr Clark tripped on a worn patch and came crashing down.

Mr and Mrs Clark seemed to fade and wear out almost in time to the fading of their possessions. I can remember some discussion about installing a modern kitchen but it never happened. Old people hate change I suppose and they were getting on a bit at the end. They hated change more than most and I saw that in particular with their clothes which became increasingly patched and worn.

If Mrs Clark loved her cows, Mr Clark loved his Labrador more. He never took the dog with us in the car when we went shooting or when we went out to run pheasants over but he insisted on letting the dog spend the night in his room. And I know from the state of the bed that the dog slept in it and under the covers.

Mr Clark also had a slightly disgusting habit of carrying bits of raw meat in his pocket and every now and then throughout the day he would take a piece out and feed his dog. Of course the constant presence of treats made the dog stick to him and when we set off anywhere in the car and left the dog behind it howled as if it was being murdered.

Mr Clark wasn't exceptional in his obsession with his dog. People I knew who worked for country aristocrats often noticed that they much preferred their dogs to their spouses and children.

With the war over, the years passed quietly for us in

Hertfordshire, but being a servant – I never kidded myself I was anything else – had gradually become almost an embarrassment. I felt like a leftover from a past where the old rules still applied. In the house the cook, housekeeper and lady's maid were all very wary of me, for example. I don't think they were wary because I was particularly stern or aloof. It was more habit than anything because, like me, they'd grown up in an era when the butler was the scary chap who hired and fired and wandered around with a face like an iron mask. We were each playing a part, you see. We were all living as if it was still 1910. The maids who came in from the village, the housekeeper and the cook and lady's maid were older than me – in their sixties or older I would have said. In fact Mrs Clark and her maid had been girls together.

The lady's maid was a bit wary with me even though, in terms of status, she was equal to or above me. I think this may have been because I was particularly good at seeming to be inscrutable – someone said that to me once and I had to look the word up, but it's probably about right.

Most of the time Mr Clark was just dotty and eccentric but occasionally he would fly into a terrible rage, usually over something fairly innocent. He never lost his temper badly with me but when he couldn't find the right trousers one morning – or perhaps what he thought were the right trousers – you could hear his screams in France. He got so mad that he threw shirts and socks and coats out of his bedroom window down on to the lawn and all the while cursing like a navvy. I waited for an hour or so and then picked the clothes up from the lawn and took them back to his room. He was still there, but sitting quietly in an old armchair.

'Would you like these in the wardrobe, sir?' I asked.

'Good lord, where did you find those?' he asked. 'I've been looking for them everywhere.'

That was the disconnected way he had of carrying on but perhaps he too was just playing a part and he really knew full well that I knew he'd thrown everything out the window in a rage.

He lost control completely on only two occasions and on one of these I think he might have committed murder if I had not intervened.

Chapter 38

It was a sunny spring day some years after the war had ended. Those who remember the countryside in the late 1940s and early 1950s will recall how quiet it all suddenly seemed after the frenzy of troop and munitions movements during hostilities. The country was virtually bankrupt, food was rationed and none of us had the money to go out – and what was there to go out to? After the war, the theatres and cinemas were still damaged or closed for lack of business and in rural districts the general lack of money was felt by all, even the wealthy.

I knew that Mr Clark was in some financial trouble. We hadn't had a pay rise for some time. The car was used much less often, even for pheasant killing. The gardener came only intermittently and the house hadn't been painted in years. Everything seemed very drab and run-down and only an occasional visitor broke the monotony. Alice and I were happy in our cottage, or at least as happy as anyone could be during those gloomy years.

Anyway, I was working in the old butler's pantry polishing the silver, a tradition we still kept up, when I looked out the window and saw a young man dressed in pale trousers and a tweed coat. He walked confidently towards the front door carrying a leather bag and he had the look of someone who was used to using the front door.

I assumed one of Mr and Mrs Clark's relatives had come to stay, but this was odd as I would normally always know in advance if anyone was expected. The young man gave a loud confident knock on the door. I opened it and said, 'Good morning, sir, how can I help you?'

Thirty years earlier no butler in England would have answered the door in a properly run house, but the old system was dying and secretly I rather liked the fact that I sometimes helped by doing the footman's job or helped out in the garden or sat and talked to the cook while she baked a pie.

'I've come to see my long-lost uncle,' said the young man with a smile. His smile was attractive enough but he had terrible skin, pockmarked and unhealthy-looking, and though he was young he was rapidly losing his thin blond hair.

'Would you like to wait a moment, sir, and I will tell Mr Clark you are here?'

'Good-oh,' he replied.

'What name shall I say?'

'It's James – Jim. He'll remember me.'

I took his coat. No hat. By the 1950s younger

people were wearing hats rather less than they should – to the scandal of the older generation.

Mr Clark, who still occasionally wore his Jaeger suits, was in the drawing room. He sat in one armchair by the window while his dog sat in the other. Both looked up as, having knocked, I came in and nodded slightly by way of a bow. Mrs Clark at this time in the morning was always downstairs dealing with the cows' milk.

'Your nephew Mr James is here, sir,' I said.

'What?' said Mr Clark.

Now this was one of Mr Clark's odd habits. He always said 'What?' when I spoke to him even though there was absolutely nothing wrong with his hearing. He liked to have everything repeated just out of habit.

'Your nephew Mr James, he is here,' I replied.

A look of puzzlement came over Mr Clark's face. He looked down at the carpet and said nothing. Half a minute or more passed. He looked out of the window and pulled a very greasy-looking sausage from the pocket of his trousers and threw it across at the dog.

'Shall I tell him you will see him, sir?' I eventually asked.

By way of reply Mr Clark got up and walked up and down while the dog, too fat to get out of its chair, watched his every movement.

'No,' he eventually said. 'I will see him later. Would you show him to the garden room?'

The garden room was one of the bedrooms that

looked over the garden at the back of the house. It was oddly named because there were several bedrooms that overlooked the garden on the same side of the house and the garden room was the smallest of these.

I made my way back down the staircase and found the young man sitting on one of those hard chairs that people always used to keep in the hall. Most wooden chairs had a sort of scalloped seat that made it at least look as if it made some concessions to human anatomy, but not hall chairs. They might have elaborately carved backs but their seats were always flat just to make sure you didn't plan on sitting on them for too long.

I showed the young man to the garden room and left him. The days when all visitors were valeted if they arrived without their own man were long over and the world had changed. This young man would probably have thought I was mad if I'd stayed to unpack his suitcase. So, after explaining that Mr Clark would see him later I left him to his own devices.

Twenty minutes later, I was taking morning tea up to the drawing room when I heard thumps and scufflings from that part of the house where Mrs Clark spent most of her time when she was not with her cows – and at this time in the morning she was always with her cows so this was something of a mystery. When I investigated I found young Mr James going through a chest of drawers in a storeroom where broken furniture, old pictures and various odds and ends were stored.

'Can I help you, sir?' I asked.

The young man turned towards me and didn't seem in the least surprised to see me nor to be discovered where he should not have been. I tried to look serious without looking accusing. I had to be careful as he was, after all, a part of the family.

'I stayed here often as a child and I'm just wondering if some of the things I used to have about me were still here. This was always a storeroom, you know, but it used to have some marvellous things in it – and I can't find any of them now!'

I nodded and left him.

'Luncheon is at one o'clock,' I said as I turned to leave.

In all my years with Mr and Mrs Clark I had never met or heard of this young man so I felt I might have to mention his odd antics to my employer. An awkward situation as I did not want to be seen to be telling tales on a family member.

I went home at lunchtime – servants' lunchtime I mean – and talked to Alice about young Jim. I had always taken every problem home to Alice over the years and her clear way of looking at things was always a great help. Nine times out of ten I took her advice.

'Just let Mr Clark know that his nephew seems to have lost something and is looking here and there for it. That way it won't look as if you're telling tales but you'll still be able to let Mr Clark know something slightly odd is happening'.

That was a typical piece of good advice from Alice and it was typical of her practical approach to everything. For years she had looked after Marjorie and me in a way that made it always a pleasure to be home. Marjorie once said, 'Mummy is always fun, isn't she?' and she was right. Everyone wants to be with someone who is positive about life in general and that was Alice all over. We didn't have the sort of money Mr Clark had but his gloomy, grubby old house wasn't a patch on our little cottage. A house reflects how happy the people in it are. That was what Alice said and that was why the big house always had a gloomy, unhappy air. Unhappiness became lodged in the pictures and furniture, in the paint and wallpaper. Mr and Mrs Clark didn't just live separate lives, they breathed separate air and the house suffered as a result. Because we were happy our little house was always bright and welcoming. I knew this was true when Alice told me one day that Mrs Clark had been coming down to the cottage once or twice a week in the morning to stay for a talk and a cup of tea.

'Do you know what's really funny about it?' asked Alice. 'The poor old thing almost looked embarrassed the first few times that she was even talking to me. Now she talks all the time and we sit together.'

Now this astonished me because in all the years I'd worked for the couple I'd hardly heard two words out of Mrs Clark, who seemed only to live through her cows. She slipped like a ghost through the big house, but according to Alice she talked her head off when they had tea together.

Alice had never really missed her days as a maid but I think our quiet life in Hertfordshire sometimes left her feeling a little bored. She never really showed it but she loved to go on holiday and with the better terms I had now – I had two weeks off each year – we would take ourselves off in summer to the seaside. Like many poorly educated people in those days abroad was just too much for us. We just thought we'd never manage; it was horribly expensive as there were no cheap flights and we could never have afforded a car or managed the language. Too timid, too, I suppose but never mind: we went to Margate and Whitstable instead. Later on, whenever I grumbled to Alice that we had never been abroad she would say, 'But how much more we did than our parents,' which was true. My father and mother hardly ever left the estate in all their years and never for a holiday.

Young Mr James and Mr Clark had lunch together that first day and they seemed to get on well. I stood in my place against the wall and, as usual, pretended to be invisible but I heard their curious conversation. The first thing I discovered was that James wasn't Mr Clark's nephew at all but a more distant relation. I couldn't quite work out what the relationship was but they seemed to have trouble recalling anything they might have had in common so the conversation was very strange.

Mr Clark said, 'How's your mother?'

James replied, 'Oh, she's dead.'

'And your brothers?'

'My sister lives in Devon and she is fine, thank you.'

There followed a long silence. James had been nodding at me at intervals to refill his glass but we were drinking one of Mr Clark's favourite wines, a rare and very expensive claret, and at the third nod from James I caught Mr Clark's eye and he very subtly shook his head so I had to pretend not to have seen Mr James's nod. It was very awkward. Luckily the meal was soon over and they retired to the drawing room together but still having said almost nothing.

I normally finished work at eight or at the latest nine and then wandered back across to the cottage for a late supper with Alice after Marjorie had gone to bed. I was about to set off for home – indeed I was halfway across the yard – when I heard a terrible crashing noise in the house. I nipped back through the door and followed the sounds to the drawing room. The row grew louder and there was shouting and the noise of breaking furniture. I opened the door and there, rolling on the floor, were Mr Clark and his nephew.

Though rather elderly Mr Clark was still a strong man and by luck or whatever he had managed to fall on top of James. He now had his hands around James's throat and the young man was very red in the face. There was nothing for it but to intervene. I didn't have time to think but I ran across to them and seized

Mr Clark's wrists. In an instant he loosened his grip and rolled off his victim. I stood up and stared, amazed that this could be happening in a house where for years nothing much had ever happened. I was so surprised I didn't really even have time to feel embarrassment. Mr Clark heaved himself upright and walked out of the room. James, who had definitely got the worst of the encounter, was sitting up but looked uncomfortable so I asked him if he would like a glass of water. He nodded and I left the room. When I returned with a glass of water he had recovered himself to some extent but he took the glass with a shaking hand and he grimaced as he swallowed. Half an hour later he had left the house. I never discovered what the two had been fighting about. Next day it was as if he had never been with us.

Chapter 39

In many ways my days now were just a more relaxed version of the traditional butler's day. I kept the wine book up to date and checked the stock in the cellar, turning some of the bottles regularly according to the whim of Mr Clark. Then I would clean the silver but no longer every week. I would chat on far more friendly terms than in the old days with the other staff. The rest of my day consisted of occasionally answering the door to the vicar or one of Mr Clark's more prominent neighbours, waiting at table and attending in the sitting room and drawing room in the evenings. We still had log fires so that was quite a job too. We had the logs delivered and an odd-job man carted them upstairs, but in the absence of a footman I had to make sure all the fires were lit and kept going in winter.

We were part of a generation that felt jobs would last forever and this was particularly true in families such as the one I'd been part of as a child. No one would ever have believed that a great estate might be broken up and sold, the house demolished and the cottages auctioned. But it happened all the time now and all over the country. I remember regularly seeing the auctioneers' notices in the paper. By the time I'd reached old age the estate I grew up on was built over – rows and rows of semi-detached houses and nothing left to see where the field tracks and the massive oaks in the park had once been. Even the lakes and ponds were filled in. I think an old gatehouse survived for a while, but in the late 1960s that too vanished.

When you read about these things happening else-where it's impossible to imagine that suddenly they might affect you personally in the here and now. Working for Mr and Mrs Clark we assumed that things would just go on as they had always gone on and the idea that we might lose job and house over-night was unimaginable. Until it happened.

Chapter 40

By 1954 Mr Clark's hunting and shooting days were long over. He had suffered a stroke and was confined to bed for months before he went off to a nursing home. Mrs Clark decided to sell up, so Alice, Marjorie and I found ourselves facing homelessness.

We had a few weeks to spare before it was time to leave and in many ways those weeks were the strangest of my life. It was as if not just our lives but the whole world had shifted and I had a feeling that the old jobs in these big country houses had come to an end for everyone of our generation. Most servants were middle-aged or older at this time and their employers were the last generation to have grown up in a world where servants were as much a part of daily life as lunch and bedtime. As the employers died or sold up so the employees were left high and dry. I read about the new breed of butlers and servants who were paid a great deal more than we were and treated almost as if they were working in an office. By that I mean their personal lives were their own and no employer would have dared to interfere in where they went during their time off or who they went with. That was the biggest change from my youth to my middle and old age, and I was lucky because after I lost my job with Mr Clark I was able to get a taste of life as a modern butler: a butler who works for new money rather than old; a butler who works for a man who has made his money rather than inherited it.

As I was soon to discover, this had both advantages and disadvantages.

Losing your home is a frightening prospect when you have no experience of finding somewhere to live because the house or the living quarters have always come with the job. As ever Alice was good and practical and of course she refused to panic. She said: 'Let's try an agency. We're not too old to change and we mustn't think we'll only get something worse than this – we might get something better!'

So off I traipsed to London to an agency.

What worried me was not that they would have no work but that I would be offered something in a new part of the country. As it turned out I needn't have worried because in the 1950s, despite the gloom of austerity, Britain did have new millionaires. Americans were still falling in love with what they saw as the old country and instead of buying old houses and rebuilding them in America they were coming over here and buying old houses and living here. Other rich people were buying flats and houses in Mayfair and Kensington because property was so cheap then. I remember seeing a massive house in central London being sold for £500.

A decade after the Second World War had ended London still looked terrible. Houses were still blackened with soot from the coal fires which weren't banned until 1963 and there were bomb sites everywhere. But here and there the rich were enjoying themselves amid the gloom and in many ways they were enjoying themselves far more than they might have otherwise precisely because most people were in the dumps. Just as in the 1920s, so now in the 1950s people wanted to forget the war and with everything so cheap and run-down those with money could really go wild. And they did.

My experience clearly stood me in good stead because the agency quickly sent me for an interview in a tall, thin, terraced house in Mayfair. I had three interviews in that house and each time I was asked the same questions by a rather large American woman called Susie. She responded to almost everything I said with the word 'Gee,' which made it very difficult to keep a straight face despite all my years playing the solemn, serious servant.

I'd never met an American at close hand before and I found it difficult to concentrate on what was being said because I knew she'd say 'gee' after each of my answers. I was also fascinated by her accent which was very strong. I later discovered that she was from Texas. Our conversation went something like this:

'Your references are excellent, Mr Sharpe, but do you know about wine, I mean French wine?'

'I do indeed, madam,' I replied. 'English gentlemen pride themselves on their cellars.'

'Gee. Do you know about German wine?'

'To a more limited extent, madam.'

'Gee. Well's that's OK. Suppose hock?'

'Hock. Exactly madam.'

'Gee. Swell. We have high expectations, Mr Sharpe. I wonder, can you assure me that you can cope with the very different standards required by an American who holds a very senior position in his government?'

I could not help resenting her line of questioning because it seemed to suggest that British employers, however grand or wealthy or both, were as nothing to a pure-blooded American. But I was very good at staying calm and the salary on offer was really very good. I stayed aloof and calm in my best butler fashion – and I got the job.

Before the First World War servants were looked down on simply for having no social status. After the Second we were looked down on for being part of an outdated system that propped up the old establishment. Servants were a throwback to feudal days it seemed, but among Americans, who were restarting their love affair with Europe, servants seemed more like Rolls Royces, and butlers were top of their shopping lists.

After my interviews with Susie I met my new employer, who astonished me at my first interview.

'Hi, you must be Bob,' he said. 'I'm Dick. He shook my hand and put his arm round my shoulders and then sat me on a huge sofa next to him. He offered me a cigarette.

He then told me all about himself at great and detailed length, even to the point of discussing his wife.

'I'll be frank with you, Bob,' he said, 'Mrs Rawlins and I do not get along. No sir. We do not. But I don't want that to worry you. If she gives you hell, and she may, I will give her hell. Yes indeed.'

'I quite understand, sir,' I said.

'I know we're going to get along swell,' he said. 'We're about the same. Yes sir we have a lot in common.'

I thought all this was wonderful and it was comforting to know that American employers were likely to be quite as eccentric as English employers but I will say it for Mr Rawlins, he was friendly – he was always very friendly. In the years I worked for him before I finally retired I don't think he ever spoke an angry word to me. He really did think we were alike, although I never quite worked out why! I think it was partly that his family had gone to America from the west of Ireland and his ancestors had been incredibly poor – as I'd been as a child.

He would often ask me up to the sitting room on the first floor of the house and say, 'Sit down, Bob. Get me a drink and get yourself one. I need someone to talk to. Mrs Rawlins has started in on me again. Does your wife start in on you? Come on, Bob, sit over here, you don't need to stand up all the time. You're giving me neck ache looking up at you.'

So I'd sit and tell him about Alice and although at first I was slightly irritated by old Rawlins I softened after a bit because you couldn't help but like him. I realised that I was being a bit sniffy about him just because he was so different from anyone else I'd worked for. We're all such conservatives, and we get more conservative as we get older.

When his important friends were coming round for dinner Mr Rawlins would say, 'Come on, Bob, it's time to play-act. It's not just one American idiot you have to deal with tonight. It's four, so I'd like to apologise in advance for my countrymen. Can you do the whole stern-faced dignified butler act – they'll love it. And don't worry. The dragon Rawlins' – he meant Mrs Rawlins – 'is out tonight.'

It was a few weeks after I started work for Mr Rawlins that I finally met Mrs Rawlins. I think I was almost shaking in my well-polished shoes when the phone rang in the flat that Alice and I had at the top of the house and a voice I hadn't heard before said,

'Hi, Bob.'

'Yes.'

'It's Mrs R. The dragon,' she laughed. 'How are ya?'

'I'm very well, thank you,' I replied in my most solemn tones.

'Do you have a moment to come down and we can get to know each other while my terrible husband is out?'

'Of course, madam,' I replied.

I trotted down the stairs, knocked on the main sitting room door and entered. Mrs Rawlins stood before me, beaming, and held out her hand. For the next ten minutes, just like her husband, she rattled away and told me all about herself. She apologised now and then for her husband, who, she said, 'talks all the time about stuff no one wants to hear. But you take no notice of him,' she said. 'If he gives you any trouble just let me know. Now I have some girls coming over to dinner in a couple of days so I want you to really do the English butler thing. Is that OK? Can you do that?'

'I can indeed, madam,' I replied.

Mr Rawlins would occasionally insist that I accompany him to the swimming baths.

'It's got to be part of your job to exercise, Bob,' he used to say. 'I need a man who knows the deep end from the shallow end.'

What on earth did that mean? I wondered.

Well, going swimming with him was an eye-opener I can tell you. We went to one of those old-fashioned pools where all the men changed together in the same room and so it was rather a shock to me after so many years as a domestic servant to find I had to get undressed – completely undressed – in front of my boss. If someone had told me thirty years earlier that such a thing could ever have happened I'd have thought him mad.

And all the time we changed into our swimming things Mr Rawlins talked. In fact he hardly seemed to need to draw breath.

'The thing about Americans, Bob, is that we're open. We're open about everything. We don't have secrets like you Europeans. I don't mean you, Bob. We're straight and when we make friends, we make friends for life, Bob, for life, and we're friends now aren't we, Bob?'

'Indeed we are, sir,' I would reply.

The more formal I was with Mr Rawlins the more friendly he tried to be. And Mrs Rawlins was just the same – except she didn't ask me to go swimming with her!

In the pool itself I lost all my dignity because I had always been a rather poor swimmer and Rawlins was good. So I would stand in the shallow end and he would slowly go up and down exchanging a nod or two with me each time he reached the shallow end where I stood trying to look wise and trying not to shiver.

'What do you think of my stroke, Bob?' he would say as he passed me.

'Very good, sir,' I would reply.

'Learned it in the desert.'

'Indeed, sir.'

He would gradually disappear towards the deep end where I never ventured. Each time he completed a length and returned to the shallow end he would say something to me.

'What would you say to a cocktail, Bob, when we're done?'

'An excellent idea, sir,' I would reply. And all the while I would try to stand in the shallow end and look like a butler, which was no easy task.

When Mr Rawlins had guests he would often tell me which ones to be snooty with.

'Look down your nose at George,' he would say. 'The man's a pain in the neck.'

When he said in the pool that we should go for a cocktail afterwards he really meant it. We would drive – his chauffeur at the wheel – to an expensive hotel and have a drink together in the bar as if we were old friends. What a contrast to those drinks I had in the local servants' pubs back in the 1920s and 1930s. But I must admit I never felt completely comfortable with this level of intimacy. I was too set in my ways I suppose. But one thing I will say for Mr Rawlins was that he was very helpful when Marjorie, my daughter, wanted to go to America some years later. He found her a job in New York and somewhere to stay. So for all his eccentricities I was always grateful to him.

Our flat at the top of the Mayfair house was lovely and Alice enjoyed living in such an interesting part of

London. In the 1950s and 1960s Mayfair was still mostly residential but it was also close to Oxford Street and Regent Street and Alice confessed to me after a few months back in London that she was happier than she had ever been. I said, 'Is that because I am more interesting and loveable than ever?'

She laughed and said, 'Sorry, it's not you – it's the shops! It's so lovely to be back where there are shops.' Much as she had liked our cottage in the countryside she felt that now she was back in London she was truly at home.

'It's like being back in Regent's Park,' she said, 'but look at the all the fun we can have. Not like in the 1930s when we couldn't go in the posh shops – now we can go wherever we like!'

It was as if we'd been in a time capsule out in the countryside and when we returned to the world everything had changed – and for the better. Our flat looked out over the rooftops and though we didn't have a garden any more it didn't matter because we had parks, including, not so far away, the park where we'd first walked together all those years ago.

When we went back to London it was as if Alice had taken ten years off her age. We went out somewhere or other every Sunday because I had so much more time off. Mr Rawlins gave me two evenings a week off and every Sunday which was an unheard-of luxury. So the wheel had come full circle. There we were again walking the streets we'd known thirty years earlier. Not a single horse was to be seen except the cavalry in the park. Many of the pre-war land-marks we knew had gone and there were still gaps from bomb damage in the rows of houses. There was an air of optimism and for ordinary people the world was certainly better now than it had ever been. You could feel it in the air. And there was no going back. If the old country estates had gone, which was sad, the old attitudes had also gone, which was a good thing because the children of the poor no longer had to grow up with a sense that they were somehow auto-matically inferior, that they had one thing only to look forward to – which was life below stairs.

Of course some of the old attitudes were still there and we were still referred to as common but people hid their views more. Looking down on people began to reflect badly on those who did it. The 1960s became, in a way, an age of equality though of course some would always be more equal than others.

We were happy in our flat, which had a gas cooker and, wonder of wonders, central heating. This was an unheard-of luxury that we never tired of smiling at each other about. We used to go to bed in winter and say, 'What about the heating? Shall we leave it on?' And Alice would say, 'I think we should. It'll be like being on holiday.' And after all the cold, damp houses we'd lived in it was glorious.

Mr Rawlins used to go away once or twice a year for a week or two and he would say, 'Just do as you please while I'm gone. Have the run of the house.'

We didn't take him at his word but I'm sure he

would not have minded if we'd parked ourselves in his part of the house for the duration. Old servants' habits die hard though, and our little flat was more than enough for us.

Chapter 41

It's curious how the days go on, passing more quickly as we get older, until a huge gulf seems to have opened between where we are now and where we once were. So much time seemed to have passed when I looked at it from one angle and so little when I looked at it from another. It was as if I'd blinked and forty years had vanished. The future just kept coming towards us and there seemed no reason to worry about it. Alice and I had occasional rows now and then and she threw a pot at my head once or twice – and she was a tremendously accurate thrower – but I probably deserved it and it was impossible anyway to imagine life without her. Then one day in the way these things happen she was no longer there. She'd been feeling tired for a few weeks, perhaps a month or two, and had stopped going out. We thought it was just old age catching up with us. Then she began to feel sick almost continually. She was sent to St Thomas's and a consultant told us the news. Alice had leukaemia. Six months later she died. It was the sort of runaway cancer that responds to no treatment and in the early 1960s – Alice died in 1962 – treatments for cancer were limited. She remained happy and positive through her last months. Each time she fell asleep she thought she would wake again and I always comfort myself with the thought that the last time she fell asleep she was not afraid because she was so sure she would wake again. She was an optimist to the last.

My overwhelming feeling after she died was not sadness but a sort of disbelief that Alice, wherever she had gone, had had the bloomin' cheek to leave me behind. For a year and more after she died I found myself at odd moments wandering round the kitchen of our flat asking Alice absent-mindedly where she'd left various things. I suppose this is common when someone you have known for a long time suddenly vanishes. It wasn't really as if she was dead at all. It was as if she had gone out and forgotten to come back.

I spent a lot of time day dreaming and thinking of the past, of the smiling girl who had come down the steps of that house in Regent's Park all those years ago. She seemed too important not to be there any more and, increasingly as I grew older, I thought of her as she had been long ago, not as she was in the final, dreadful months of her life as she shrank before my eyes.

The past before Alice came back to me too: the fields of the old estate and fishing with my brother; the maids at the big house, the bells ringing from the great rooms and the long stone corridors and old pictures on the walls and carts in the yard. But like Alice, the carts and pictures, the stone corridor and the great rooms were all gone.

I think I rather lost heart after Alice died, although Mr Rawlins gave me as much time as I needed. Eighteen months later I decided to retire. It was an odd decision really as I had no plans to do anything in particular, my duties were minimal and my pay generous. But the heart had gone out of me.

In those days it was still possible to get a privately rented flat that had what was called a controlled rent. It was a flat for people who could not afford to buy somewhere or pay a market rent. A very good system if you ask me. Mr Rawlins gave me a letter saying that my employment with him would end shortly and I would be homeless, which was no less than the truth. I was offered a council flat but hated the look of it. Then through a contact Mr Rawlins found me a private, rent-controlled flat in Paddington. I signed a contract that ensured the rent would never go up more than a few shillings a year and I settled down to retirement.

It was the first time in my life I had been completely free and though I missed so many aspects of my years in service I was never bored or at a loss. My retirement would have been far happier with Alice, of course, but I didn't mope or give up because Alice would not have wanted it. She'd have laughed and given me a shove and said, 'Come on, lots to do, look sharp!'

When I look back I never think that my life below stairs was a wasted life. No, I think that if I hadn't been in service I might never have met Alice and with Alice no life could ever be wasted.